THE
ALFRED HITCHCOCK
TRIVIOGRAPHY &
QUIZ BOOK

THE
ALFRED HITCHCOCK
TRIVIOGRAPHY &
QUIZ BOOK

Kathleen Kaska

RENAISSANCE BOOKS
Los Angeles

Library of Congress Cataloging-in-Publication Data
    Kaska, Kathleen.
        Alfred Hitchcock triviography & quiz book / Kathleen Kaska.
            p.   cm.
        Filmography: p.
        Videography: p.
        Includes bibliographical references and index.
        ISBN 1-58063-070-7 (pbk. : alk. paper)
            1. Hitchcock, Alfred, 1899–   —Miscellanea. 2. Motion pictures—
    Miscellanea. I. Title. II. Title: Alfred Hitchcock triviography and quiz book.
    PN1998.3.H58K37   1999
    791.43'0233'092—dc21   99-21727
                                                                                CIP

10 9 8 7 6 5 4 3 2 1

Design by Susan Shankin

Distributed by St. Martin's Press
Manufactured in the United States of America
First Edition

This book is dedicated to

Ted and Marcella Kaska;

with special thanks to Lloyd—

my very own L. B. Jeffries.

acknowledgments

I am grateful to the following people who assisted me in my research: Dian Donnell (owner) and W. Craig Pankey (general manger) of Vulcan Video, and Murray Messelt, owner of The Movie Store, for the use of their extensive collections of Alfred Hitchcock videos; Linda Nesenholtz, Martha Medlock, and Ruth Carter for their proofreading and editing; my agent Peter Rubie for his expert counsel; editor Jim Parish for his valuable advice; and Lloyd Broussard for his encouragement and constant support.

contents

THE
ALFRED HITCHCOCK
TRIVIOGRAPHY &
QUIZ BOOK

CHAPTER I

The master of suspense

"Now, this brings us to suspense,

which is the most powerful means of holding

onto the viewer's attention."

ALFRED HITCHCOCK, 1967

INTERTWINING THE NUANCES OF SUSPENSE AND SURPRISE, Alfred Hitchcock (1899–1980) always kept his audience on the edge of its seats—right where he wanted them. Hitchcock/Truffaut (1983), by François Truffaut, details Hitchcock's views on the difference between these two elements, and how their proper use made a thriller into a triumphant work of art. Hitchcock's technique was knowing what specifically to tell an audience and when. For sufficient surprise, he felt the audience should know very little about what was to occur. In his conversations with Truffaut, Hitchcock gave the example of a bomb exploding without any warning. There was no anticipation of the event. It just happened, and the audience then had to deal with its bewilderment. Surprise alone did not make a thriller more clever, unless it was utilized as a twist at the end.

On the other hand, Hitchcock felt that suspense took place when the audience was aware a bomb was near and an explosion was imminent. The sequential developments were always revealed to the audience as they unfolded, but the characters in the film were oblivious. The inability to warn the characters of their fate made the audience feel completely powerless. However, it also put the audience into the story by creating an intimacy between themselves and the screen characters. Nevertheless, being unable to help, the audience could only watch the event unfold before their eyes. This technique was utilized in many of Hitchcock's films: in *Easy Virtue* (1927), the suspense was in an offer of marriage made while a telephone operator listened intently for the woman's reply; while in *Rear Window* (1954), the audience held its breath as the villain of the piece, Thorwald, entered his apartment while the heroine, Lisa, was searching his bedroom for clues to a possible murder.

Alfred Hitchcock's masterful weaving of these elements of suspense and surprise always gave his audience bone-chilling thrills, before flattening them with his typical shocking endings. Chapter 1 also presents other elements for which Hitchcock is famous: innovative technique, witty dialogue, memorable scenes, and, of course, his signature cameo appearances. Other chapters cover each of the films he directed (with the exception of the silent film, *The Mountain Eagle*, 1925, of which no print is known to exist, and the only musical Hitchcock ever directed, *Waltzes from Vienna*, 1933), his television career, and his life in general. Some items will be familiar and others will be more difficult to identify. Nonetheless, the quizzes are sure to rekindle the surprise and suspense encountered from viewing these classic films and TV shows. In solving them, you may even hear a faint echo: "Straaaaange, isn't it?"

QUIZ **I**

Film Plots:
The Moral of the Story

Most of Hitchcock's films convey the struggles of good versus evil, right versus wrong, and contrast the bizarre with the mundane aspects of life. Filmmaker François Truffaut described Hitchcock's films as having three crucial elements: fear, sex, and death. The moral aspect of each theme prevails—the good guy usually overcomes evil and evil does not go unpunished. The following quiz summarizes the plots of twenty Alfred Hitchcock feature films. See if you can name the correct title of each movie from its summary.

1. This newlywed's lack of self-confidence was a bit daunting. She allowed the possessions of her husband's first wife to remain in the house and the servants to intimidate her, and she hid behind the door while the first wife's lover roamed about at his leisure. Her cowering role was emphasized by her not having a first name in the story. However, good triumphed over evil, and in the face of danger and destruction, her inner strength emerged at the end. Rebecca

2. Some married couples vow never to go to bed angry. However, David and Ann resolved never to leave the bedroom *until* their quarrels were over. Their record for self-confinement was six days. Yet the resolution of their most recent marital conflict was confounding, because reconciliation required not only leaving the bedroom, but making a trip back to the altar.

3. Superior-class idealism, Nietzschean philosophy, and the right to commit murder for the privileged few—all hypothetically, that is—were

elements that made for an interesting dinner party conversation. Or was it *just* conversation? Brandon's party plan seemed to be going extremely well, from the cold chicken to the candelabras. So where did he go wrong? *Rope* ✓

4. Did Lina finally take her nose out of her psychology book long enough to let her imagination run away with her? When she first met Johnny she was willing to overlook his faults. However, the honeymoon was soon over. She began suspecting her husband of trying to swindle and then murder his best friend. Besides, she became convinced that Johnny was going to poison her for the insurance money.

5. A child can be such a nuisance, especially when the mother is trying to concentrate on winning a skeet-shooting contest and the youngster is in the background chattering away. Mother's stray shot caused the trophy to go to someone else. However, mom's inattention quickly sang a different tune when her child was kidnapped; and this time her aim was true. *The Man Who* ✓

6. Alicia wanted nothing more than to give up her life of partying to settle down with her new lover. However, she had agreed to help her country, even if it meant forsaking her lover and marrying an enemy. The situation soon veered out of control, and Alicia's first assignment was almost her last.

7. Johnny, a.k.a. Huntley, wanted to get a scoop on the war situation from the front lines. He also wanted to marry Carol. Little did Johnny know that Carol was the daughter of the enemy spy ring's leader, and that the enemy had the scoop on him.

8. Marion was looking for a private island, but fell into a private trap instead. Ironically, it was her captor who helped her to realize her mistake. However, Marion did not have a chance to make amends, because her stay in limbo turned out to be a one-way ticket to hell. *Psycho* ✓

9. Barry Kane wanted desperately to clear his name of a crime he didn't commit. His quest took him on a journey from the Bicarbonate Belt

to the Big Apple, from the desert to a deserted town, from a ride in a freight truck to a jaunt in a boxcar packed with circus freaks, and from a quaint cabin in the woods to a mansion and a society ball.

10. Tony had everything arranged, right down to the last detail. He would finally be rid of his wife forever. Even when plan A failed, Tony had plan B in place before you could say, "Hide a key." However, Inspector Hubbard was convinced that Tony's wife was innocent and set a trap for Tony. *Dial M for Murder*

11. As they say, "You scratch my back and I'll scratch yours." Bruno thought it would be the perfect plan to get rid of his interfering father: murder without any motive. Yet, all Guy wanted was a divorce. He had no intention of having his wife killed. *SO A T*

12. Scottie and Judy's relationship was doomed from the beginning: Judy was married to one man, but was another man's mistress; she committed suicide but was also murdered. Then, to top it all off, Judy was, in fact, a different woman than Scottie suspected. *Vertigo*

13. If you drive that breathtaking route up Highway 1 north of San Francisco, you'll pass through Bodega Bay. The schoolhouse is still there and so are the avian silhouettes in the window, but the children are nowhere in sight. *The birds*

14. L. B. gave a new meaning to the phrase "Peeping Tom." When his binoculars proved ineffective, he graduated to a 400-millimeter telephoto lens. For those hard-to-see corners across the way, he engaged his nurse and girlfriend in some hands-on snooping. *RW*

15. Living in small-town America bored dear Charlie to tears. Her family was stuck in a rut and life offered little excitement. Nonetheless, Charlie decided to make something happen. She invited her namesake uncle for a visit, and her entire world turned upside down. Her relative was exciting, all right. His bag of tricks contained robbery, blackmail, and murder.

16. Mark's professional life offered little challenge. Running the family business was a far cry from the fascinating zoological world of man and beast. Yet, when he decided to tame the ultimate beast he got more than he bargained for. Training a jaguarundi was simple compared to training his wife.

17. No one believed Roger's tale of abduction and espionage, not even his mother. His only recourse was to find George Kaplan and clear his name, so to speak.

18. John Robie had a difficult time losing his bad reputation. Even though he had given up his life of crime, he was still being accused of crimes he had not committed. A copycat burglar was making life difficult for him.

19. You can't keep a good man down, nor a drunken, nasty one either. He was a pain when he was alive, but he had become an even bigger problem now that he was dead.

20. Richard stepped out of the frying pan and into the fire when he left the bar from which he had been fired and sought help from his friend, a produce vendor. Richard was wanted for murder and his ex-wife became a convenient pawn in the potato sack murder scheme.

QUIZ **2**

Art and Technique:
Dark and Stormy Nights

Alfred Hitchcock's filming forte lay in his creative ability with the camera, creating scenes deemed impossible by his predecessors and often mimicked by his peers and his successors. He was also a master of expediency on the film set. For example, during the silent film era, while making a picture in Germany, Hitchcock had trouble signaling the hidden scene-shifters who were located behind the set and who, in turn, were to provide the cue for the angels (actors) to begin their routine. To solve this problem, Hitchcock fired a gun loaded with blanks every time he wanted his groups of angels to jump from their tiers. According to John Russell Taylor in his authorized biography, *Hitch* (1978), "Visitors to the set were somewhat taken aback to see the usually mild, peaceable Hitchcock running up and down, apparently threatening his angels with a pistol and getting them to jump to his orders with a plentiful expenditure of blanks." In the following quiz, match the twenty different camera techniques with the movie in which they were used.

1. A luminous bulb was placed in a glass of milk, causing the glass to draw the attention of the audience.
   A. *The Lady Vanishes*   B. *Rebecca*
   C. *Suspicion*   D. *Vertigo*

2. The camera setup was designed to swing around the characters as the furniture and walls rolled out of the way. This technique allowed for long, continuous ten-minute sequence shots. The camera was in perpetual movement, avoiding typical scene cuts.
   A. *Dial M for Murder*   B. *Marnie*
   C. *The Paradine Case*   D. *Rope*

3. Hitchcock often experimented with innovative movie techniques. This feature film was shot in 3-D.
   A. *Dial M for Murder*   B. *Rear Window*
   C. *Strangers on a Train*   D. *The Trouble with Harry*

4. Hitchcock used the fade-out technique in this movie to indicate passage of time and the conclusions of acts, a film convention which he rarely employed.
   A. *Frenzy*   B. *Rear Window*
   C. *The Secret Agent*   D. *Torn Curtain*

5. In this movie Hitchcock used a technique which utilized mirrors to reflect more light on the set, allowing him to film scenes of this movie in a dark, poorly lit museum.
   A. *Blackmail*
   B. *The Man Who Knew Too Much* (1934)
   C. *Spellbound*
   D. *Young and Innocent*

6. In order to offset the physically slight Claude Rains as he approached his taller leading lady, Ingrid Bergman, Hitchcock had a gradually inclining plank built on the sound stage for this screen production.
   A. *Jamaica Inn*   B. *Notorious*
   C. *Spellbound*   D. *Under Capricorn*

7. In this picture, Hitchcock filmed a plane crashing into the ocean with water rushing into the cockpit and drowning the two pilots. This was shot in a water tank using a transparency screen which tore away at the push of a button, allowing the water to come rushing in through the window. The action sequence was shot in one take, without *any* cutting and splicing.
   A. *Foreign Correspondent*   B. *Lifeboat*
   C. *Number Seventeen*   D. *The 39 Steps*

8. In this entry, a carousel appears to whirl away at a terrific speed and then comes crashing to an explosive halt. Hitchcock created this realistic scene by photo-graphing the explosion of a miniature carousel. He enlarged this piece of film and projected it onto a screen, then positioned the actors around it.
   A. *The Birds*   B. *Family Plot*
   C. *Saboteur*   D. *Strangers on a Train*

9. For one of his early screen works—filmed in 1930—Hitchcock wanted his character's inner thoughts heard over music as the character shaved in front of a mirror. To accomplish this effect the actor's voice

was previously recorded and played back. A thirty-piece live orchestra was positioned behind the bathroom wall. The music was recorded along with the actor's voice. The audience watched the actor shave and heard his voice accompanied by the background music.

A. *Champagne*

B. *Juno and the Paycock*

C. *The Man Who Knew Too Much* (1934)

D. *Murder!*

10. The homicide in this thriller was viewed indirectly through the glasses of the woman being strangled. To give this effect, Hitchcock used a large distorting lens and photographed the two actors' reflections in the glasses.

A. *Frenzy*   B. *Number Seventeen*

C. *Strangers on a Train*   D. *Topaz*

11. In this film Hitchcock attached a camera onto England's largest crane to film a crowded ballroom, allowing the camera to descend 145 feet to within four inches of the drummer's face.

A. *Saboteur*   B. *The Secret Agent*

C. *The Skin Game*   D. *Young and Innocent*

12. Hitchcock was ready to add the final touches to this movie and pronounce it complete, when John Maxwell, executive head of British International Pictures, announced that a new sound system was ready for use. Some of the sequences were reshot providing the British film industry, as well as Alfred Hitchcock, with its first talkie.

A. *Blackmail*   B. *Champagne*

C. *Juno and the Paycock*   D. *The Manxman*

13. This film was Hitchcock's first feature shot in Technicolor.

A. *The Paradine Case*   B. *Rope*

C. *Strangers on a Train*   D. *Under Capricorn*

14. In this movie, Hitchcock had a camouflaged plastic tube filled with blood placed on the face of his actor. When the performer was "stabbed," a string was pulled, releasing the blood so it ran down the victim's face along a previously traced line.

A. *The Birds*   B. *Frenzy*

C. *Marnie*   D. *Psycho*

15. The opening scene for this film included a shot of the entrance of a Gothic cathedral with one-hundred-foot columns. Building the entire entrance would have been too time consuming and costly, so Hitchcock built one column to scale and shot it from different camera angles. The technique was very effective.

A. *Rebecca*   B. *Rich and Strange*

C. *The 39 Steps*   D. *Under Capricorn*

16. In this movie, Hitchcock used a camera suspended from a helicopter to shoot a wide-angle view of the Thames River in London. The audience was given a bird's-eye shot of the smoggy city as the camera settled on a political rally where the candidate urged the cleanup of the city's polluted environment.

A. *Frenzy*

B. *The Man Who Knew Too Much* (1956)

C. *Topaz*

D. *Torn Curtain*

17. Filming in a government building where cameras were restricted was not a problem for the ingenious Hitchcock. He secretly concealed several cameramen with their equipment to get the desired background footage for this picture.

A. *Foreign Correspondent*

B. *The Man Who Knew Too Much* (1956)

C. *North by Northwest*

D. *Notorious*

18. This costume drama was Hitchcock's second attempt at using ten-minute scene takes. However, these lengthy takes caused so much stress among the actors and crew that the scenes finally had to be shortened.

    A. *Notorious*   B. *Spellbound*

    C. *Suspicion*   D. *Under Capricorn*

19. In the opening scene of this work Hitchcock wanted a closeup of a finger dialing a phone. Unable to achieve the proper image under normal conditions, Hitchcock had a giant telephone dial and a huge wooden finger constructed in order to display the image he wanted.

    A. *Dial M for Murder*   B. *Downhill*

    C. *Number Seventeen*   D. *Strangers on a Train*

20. In this production, Hitchcock placed a sheet of glass on the face of a woman and then positioned a light behind her head so that her hair shone. The reflection resembled a woman under water. Hint: this shot was the opening scene in which the woman had drowned.

    A. *The Farmer's Wife*   B. *The Lodger*

    C. *The Manxman*   D. *Murder*

QUIZ **3**

The Cameo: Hitchcock's Signature

What started out as an immediate need for a walk-on extra to fill space on the screen turned into a Hitchcock movie tradition. Hitchcock's subtle cameo was difficult to detect in his early films; a viewer had to be very observant to catch him strolling down the street or to notice his face in a crowd. However, as Hitchcock's career progressed and his frame grew, his cameos increased and lengthened. His appearances became very noticeable, often as humorous dichotomies that mocked a character in his current movie. The following quiz features twenty-five of Hitchcock's most memorable onscreen cameos. Match the cameo with the correct film title.

CAMEO

1. Gawky photographer taking a picture of a courthouse scene

2. Passenger boarding a train carrying a bass violin

3. Spectator watching acrobats in an Arab market

4. Passenger at a train station toting a cello case

5. Man wearing a ten-gallon hat

6. Passenger leaving a London railroad station smoking a cigarette

7. Spectator at an arrest scene

8. Silhouette on a door labeled "Registrar of Births and Deaths"

9. Customer leaving Davidson's Pet Store with two dogs

10. Man coming out of a crowded elevator

11. Person missing a bus as the doors close in his cherubic face

12. Party guest gulping champagne

13. Man strolling down the street, passing a policeman

14. Guest being photographed at the dinner table during a reunion

15. Character winding a clock on a mantle as another character plays the piano

16. Man being pushed in a wheelchair by a nurse as he boards a United Airlines flight

17. Subway passenger trying to read while being pestered by a young boy

18. Individual sitting in the last seat of a crowded bus next to the leading man and a cage of birds

19. Model in a before-and-after newspaper ad for a diet product called Reduco

20. Man gawking at the narrative's leading lady as she talks to herself

21. Person in a crowd listening to a speech

22. Pedestrian passing a bus parked in front of a music hall

23. Character among a crowd of people listening to a politician speak, and, a moment later, watching the police drag a corpse from the Thames River

24. Man clutching all thirteen spades while playing bridge on a train with a doctor and his wife

25. Character sitting in a hotel lobby holding a baby on his knee

TITLE

A. *Rear Window*

B. *The Paradine Case*

C. *The Birds*

D. *Notorious*

E. *The 39 Steps*

F. *Lifeboat*

G. *Shadow of a Doubt*

H. *Spellbound*

I. *Frenzy*

J. *Rebecca*

K. *The Lady Vanishes*

L. *Under Capricorn*

M. *Dial M for Murder*

N. *Psycho*

O. *Young and Innocent*

P. *Stage Fright*

Q. *The Man Who Knew Too Much* (1956)

R. *Strangers on a Train*

S. *The Lodger*

T. *Blackmail*

U. *Topaz*

V. *Torn Curtain*

W. *Family Plot*

X. *North by Northwest*

Y. *To Catch a Thief*

QUIZ **4**

Hitchcock Quotes:
Candid and Coy

Excited over the prospect of filming *North by Northwest* (1959), Hitchcock let his stoic guard down after a few martinis with screenwriter Ernest Lehman and whispered, "Ernie, do you realize what we're doing in this picture? The audience is like a giant organ that you and I are playing. At one moment we play this note on them and get this reaction, and then we play that chord and they react that way. And someday we won't even have to make a movie—there'll be electrodes implanted in their brains, and we'll just press different buttons and they'll go 'ooooh' and 'aaaah' and we'll frighten them, and make them laugh. Won't that be wonderful?"

Hitchcock made many of the following remarks to film director François Truffaut during their conversations and interviews between 1962 and 1966. Match the following twenty Hitchcock films with their respective quotes. Film titles may be used more than once.

QUOTE

1. ". . . was an absurd thing to undertake."

2. "Since I didn't really understand the type of people who are portrayed in the film, all I did was to photograph the scenes as written."

3. "About this time I felt that my batteries were fully charged."

4. "It's a fun picture."

5. "It's not a Hitchcock picture. The story is old-fashioned [and] lacking in humor."

6. "I made that picture to prove that the American public could appreciate British humor."

7. "I made sure that the public would not be able to anticipate from one scene to another."

8. "I had no special admiration for the novel, and I don't think I would have made the picture if it hadn't been for Ingrid Bergman."

9. "I was intrigued by the hero's attempts to recreate the image of a dead woman through another one who's alive."

10. "I don't think I'm really any good at stories that are completely written by someone else. It was an entity all its own, written by Sean O'Casey, and all I could do about it was to cast it and direct the players."

11. "Find me a piece of land jutting into the sea, with a road running along it. There must be a lonely house and a jetty, and anchored off the jetty a schooner."

12. "A disaster! . . . a careless approach to my work."

13. "It contained the worst title I've ever written."

14. "I want to have one scene of a man hanging onto Lincoln's eyebrows. That's all the picture I have so far."

15. "Always a bridesmaid, never a bride."

16. "I couldn't find anyone to work on it with me. They all felt my first draft was so flat and factual that they couldn't see one iota of quality in it."

17. "I wanted to turn out the first picture on psychoanalysis."

18. "There isn't very much we can say about that one, is there? . . . I just did my job, using cinematic means to narrate a story taken from a stage play."

19. "Let's say that the first version was the work of a talented amateur and the second was made by a professional."

20. "I undertook it as a stunt . . . I got this crazy idea to do it in a single shot."

FILM

A. *Rope*	K. *The Trouble with Harry*
B. *North by Northwest*	L. *Strangers on a Train*
C. *Spellbound*	M. *Juno and the Paycock*
D. *Rebecca*	N. *Mr. and Mrs. Smith*
E. *Jamaica Inn*	O. *Stage Fright*
F. *Vertigo*	P. *Rear Window*
G. *Number Seventeen*	Q. *Under Capricorn*
H. *Psycho*	R. *Easy Virtue*
I. *Dial M for Murder*	S. *Rope*
J. *The Birds*	T. *The Man Who Knew Too Much* (1956)

QUIZ 5

Landmarks: And If You Look to Your Left . . .

Hitchcock shot several scenes using national monuments, museums, and other significant points of interest. However, because Mount Rushmore is a shrine of democracy, the U.S. government prohibits defacing the monument in any way. While filming *North by Northwest* (1959), the U.S.

Department of Interior would not allow Hitchcock to shoot any scenes which showed the presidents' faces above the chin line, even though Hitchcock was using a replica for closeup scenes of Mount Rushmore. However, with the help of art director Robert Boyle, Hitchcock arranged Cary Grant and Eva Marie Saint directly in front of Jefferson's face. Match the fifteen notable locations following with the correct film. A movie title may be used more than once.

LOCATION

1. Albert Hall (London, England)

2. Mount Rushmore (South Dakota)

3. The British Museum (London, England)

4. Statue of Liberty (New York City)

5. Old Bailey Court (London, England)

6. Covent Garden (London, England)

7. Jefferson Memorial (Washington, D.C.)

8. Grace Cathedral (San Francisco)

9. United Nations (New York City)

10. The flower gardens (Nice, France)

11. The Isle of Man (British Isles)

12. Arc de Triomphe (Paris, France)

13. Aquarium at the London Zoo (England)

14. Golden Gate Bridge (San Francisco)

15. Berlin Museum (Germany)

FILM

A. *Strangers on a Train*

B. *The Manxman*

C. *The Paradine Case*

D. *Blackmail*

E. *North by Northwest*

F. *Vertigo*

G. *Family Plot*

H. *The Man Who Knew Too Much* (1956)

I. *Torn Curtain*

J. *Topaz*

K. *To Catch a Thief*

L. *Sabotage*

M. *Saboteur*

N. *Frenzy*

QUIZ **6**

Awards and Achievements: And the Winner Is . . .

During his five decades of filmmaking Alfred Hitchcock received numerous awards and honorary degrees from organizations such as the Academy of Motion Picture Arts and Sciences and the American Film Institute. The following quiz consists of twenty multiple choice questions concerning these awards.

1. For which film was Hitchcock first nominated for Best Director by the Academy of Motion Pictures Arts and Sciences?
    A. *Lifeboat*
    C. *Rope*
    B. *Rear Window* ~
    D. *Suspicion*

2. Which literary award did Hitchcock receive for Best Mystery Writer, and for which movie?

   A. Agatha for *The Man Who Knew Too Much* (1956)

   B. Anthony for *The Birds*

   C. Edgar for *Rear Window*

   D. Macavity for *Notorious*

3. Which Golden Globe Award did Hitchcock win in 1958?

   A. Best Technical Achievement   B. Best Director

   C. Best Television Adaptation   D. Best Television Series of the Year

4. Which Hitchcock film lost first prize to *The Nun's Story* at the San Sebastian International Film Festival?

   A. *North by Northwest*   B. *Psycho*

   C. *Vertigo*   D. *The Wrong Man*

5. Which two Hitchcock-directed feature films won the Oscar for Best Cinematography from the Academy of Motion Picture Arts and Sciences?

   A. *The Paradine Case* and *Under Capricorn*

   B. *Rebecca* and *To Catch a Thief*

   C. *Shadow of a Doubt* and *The Birds*

   D. *The Trouble with Harry* and *Vertigo*

6. Which Hitchcock-directed movie won an Oscar for Best Picture?

   A. *Foreign Correspondent*   B. *Rebecca*

   C. *To Catch a Thief*   D. *Topaz*

7. How many times was Alfred Hitchcock nominated for an Oscar for Best Director?

   A. Never   B. Two

   C. Five   D. Eight

8. Which film organization honored Hitchcock with the Best Picture Award in 1938 for *The Lady Vanishes*?

   A. Golden Globe Award

   B. The Academy of Motion Picture Arts and Sciences

   C. British Society of Film and Television Arts

   D. New York Film Critics

9. Which American university awarded Hitchcock an honorary degree?
   A. Stanford University   B. Columbia University
   C. Yale University -   D. Georgetown University

10. For which film did Hitchcock receive the Golden Globe Award for "outstanding contributions to the entertainment field"?
    A. *Family Plot*   B. *Frenzy*
    C. *Marnie* -   D. *Torn Curtain*

11. In which year did the Academy of Motion Picture Arts and Sciences present Hitchcock with the Irving G. Thalberg Memorial Award "for the most consistent high level of production achievement by an individual"?
    A. 1968   B. 1970
    C. 1975   D. 1976 -

12. Which North American university awarded Hitchcock an honorary doctorate "for magnificent accomplishment in the world of cinema"?
    A. University of California at Santa Cruz
    B. University of Southern California -
    C. Boston University
    D. Harvard University

13. What trophy was bestowed upon Hitchcock by the *Photoplay* Gold Medal Awards?
    A. Best Director   B. Best Technical Achievement
    C. Special Editors' Award   D. Best Screenplay Adaptation

14. Who presented Hitchcock with the first honorary membership into the British Society of Film and Television Arts in a ceremony at the Royal Albert Hall in London in 1971?
    A. Queen Elizabeth II   B. James Stewart _
    C. Cary Grant   D. Princess Anne

15. Which city declared July 14, 1966, as "Alfred Hitchcock Day"?
    A. Oxford   B. Boston
    C. New York   D. London

16. Toward the end of Hitchcock's career which organization awarded him with the Life Achievement Award?
   A. The Academy of Motion Pictures Arts and Sciences
   B. American Film Institute
   C. Association of Cinematography, Television, and Allied Technicians
   D. The Directors Guild of Canada

17. Which prize was Hitchcock given by the British-American Chamber of Commerce in 1979?
   A. Man of the Year
   B. Best Independent Business Owner
   C. Most Honored Citizen
   D. Lifetime Achievement

18. In what year did Queen Elizabeth II of England make Alfred Hitchcock a Knight Commander of the British Empire?
   A. 1969   B. 1974
   C. 1977   D. 1980

19. On April 29, 1974, Hitchcock was honored in New York City by the Film Society of Lincoln Center. In addition to his wife, Alma, who accompanied Hitchcock to this gala event?
   A. Ingrid Bergman   B. Tippi Hedren
   C. Doris Day   D. Grace Kelly

20. Which organization presented Hitchcock with the Milestone Award in 1965 for his contributions to American motion pictures?
   A. Writers Guild of America
   B. The American Film Institute
   C. Screen Producers Guild
   D. Directors Guild of New York

QUIZ 7

Character Profiles:
The Good, the Bad, and the Scary

Many character types appear repeatedly in several Alfred Hitchcock films: spies, thieves, innocent victims, and individuals with Oedipus complexes. The following quiz includes fifteen short personality profiles in which the characters describe themselves in "their" own words. Read the descriptions and identify the characters.

1. "I am a compulsive gambler, habitual liar, and just an all-around fun guy. My wife has a bit of a problem with that, but that's just the way I am. After all, Beaky doesn't mind."

2. "I may be a gorgeous socialite, but I'm not beyond breaking and entering to prove to L. B. that I can spice up his life rather than merely tie him down with the bonds of matrimony." *Lisa Fremont*

3. "I tried to do what was right and marry the man whose proposal I accepted. But my love for Philip could not be squelched. If only Carl would have remained dead, everyone would have been much happier."

4. "My husband had a difficult time accepting the fact that I agreed to marry his best friend and business partner. But what's a girl to do when the man she married turns out to be single?"

5. "Life was getting a bit boring, so I decided to become a spy. I could travel, use an alias, and even carry a gun. This position also provided me with the opportunity to find a husband."

6. "I, like my creator, suffered from acute melancholia, together with a guilt complex. I'll be okay if I can just keep my feet on the ground."

7. "Okay, okay, I'll admit that I have a curious nature. But that's what I do for a living—observe and scrutinize. I'm a freelance photographer, and being temporarily homebound I just naturally turn my attention to my neighbors. But I've learned my lesson. Their boring little lives aren't so benign, and now I'm paying the price for spying. I'm stuck in my apartment for several more weeks." *CBJ*

8. "What a week! I was on my way to a business luncheon and my life turned upside down. Mistaken for someone else, I was kidnapped, almost murdered and run down in a cornfield by a crop duster. However, it all ended on a happy note: I found my future wife hanging off the end of a cliff at Mount Rushmore." *Guy from North by Northwest*

9. "I was doing fairly well for myself. My life was full of travel and intrigue until my boss caught me with my hand in the till and gave me an ultimatum to marry him or go to prison. I chose the altar—a big mistake. I quickly realized that marriage *was* a prison."

10. "I went into the insurance office yesterday to try and get a loan to cover my wife's dental bills. I'm a musician in New York City and I can barely scratch out a living. Well, earlier today the police arrived and arrested me for robbing several stores in my neighborhood. I'll admit that I was desperate for money, but I'm not a criminal. So here I sit in jail waiting for my relatives to post bail. I hope Rose wasn't too worried when I didn't come home for dinner last night."

11. "Just once I'd like to have a friend over for supper—a girlfriend—and not have my mother hit the ceiling. The last time I invited a lady to dinner, I had to serve our sandwiches in the office. Mother just worries about me too much. She thinks that all women are cheap and amoral. I'm a grown man, but I can't leave my mother, she is so much a part of me. Sometimes I feel like I was born into a trap." *Norman Bates*

12. "That's the last time I do a favor for a friend. He refused to keep his part of the bargain after I went to the trouble of arranging everything. He'd better not cross me again. But if he does, I have a few more tricks up my sleeve. After all, a deal's a deal."

Someone from Strangers On A Train

13. "Traveling with my mother is such a bore. She drinks too much and flirts with anything in pants. My father died and left us dripping in oil—reserves, so my mother and I have been resort-hopping. Landing on the French Riviera was heaven. I've fallen in love with a very dangerous man. We have a date for a picnic this afternoon, and I plan to offer him my services as his partner in crime." *To Catch A Thief*

14. "I'm a sucker for a man with a tattoo, and John Kovak has five. He is a bit rough around the edges, but who am I to get my nose out of joint? I'm just a broad who made it big. If we survive this ordeal, I think John and I may have a chance. We speak the same language because we're both from the South Side of Chicago."

15. "I've learned a valuable lesson this summer. Be careful what you ask for, you might just get it. I was bored to tears and hoping for some excitement to come my way. Big mistake! Three murder attempts were made on my life by a relative I loved and trusted."

Dial M?

QUIZ **8**

Casting:
Leading and Supporting Roles

Throughout his career, Alfred Hitchcock had a love/hate relationship with his cast members. He was quoted as saying, "Actors are cattle—actresses, too. I tell them I hate the sight of them and they love it, the exhibitionists!" The following quiz contains seventy-five films and sixty actors. Match the actor with the character from the correct film. Some performers are used more than once.

CHARACTER

1. Roger Thornhill in *North by Northwest*

2. Madeleine Elster in *Vertigo*

3. Johnny Jones in *Foreign Correspondent*

4. Rupert Cadell in *Rope*

5. Constance Porter in *Lifeboat*

6. Bruno Anthony in *Strangers on a Train*

7. Mitch Brenner in *The Birds*

8. Jo McKenna in *The Man Who Knew Too Much* (1956)

9. Pamela in *The 39 Steps*

10. Charlie Oakley in *Shadow of a Doubt*

11. Michael Armstrong in *Torn Curtain*

12. Norman Bates in *Psycho*

13. John Robie in *To Catch a Thief*

14. Barry Kane in *Saboteur*

15. Max de Winter in *Rebecca*

16. Henrietta Flusky in *Under Capricorn*

17. T. R. Devlin in *Notorious*

18. Jennifer Rodgers in *The Trouble with Harry*

19. Tony Wendice in *Dial M for Murder*

20. Christopher Emmanuel Balestrero in *The Wrong Man*

21. George Lumley in *Family Plot*

22. Bob Lawrence in *The Man Who Knew Too Much* (1934)

23. Kate Caesar in *The Manxman*

24. The General in *The Secret Agent*

25. Johnny Aysgarth in *Suspicion*

26. Anthony Keane in *The Paradine Case*

27. Gus in *Lifeboat*

28. Eve Kendall in *North by Northwest*

29. Lisa Carol Freemont in *Rear Window*

30. Marion Crane in *Psycho*

31. Bob Rusk in *Frenzy*

32. Marnie Edgar in *Marnie*

33. Alicia Huberman in *Notorious*

34. Mrs. de Winter in *Rebecca*

35. Squire Humphrey Pengallan in *Jamaica Inn*

36. Ann Smith in *Mr. and Mrs. Smith*

37. John Ballantine in *Spellbound*

38. Ruth Grandfort in *I Confess*

39. Frances Stevens in *To Catch a Thief*

40. Guy Haines in *Strangers on a Train*

41. Lars Thorwald in *Rear Window*

42. Lina McLaidlaw in *Suspicion*

43. Erica in *Young and Innocent*

44. Charlotte Inwood in *Stage Fright*

45. Melanie Daniels in *The Birds*

46. Michael Nordstrom in *Topaz*

47. Mark Rutland in *Marnie*

48. Margot Wendice in *Dial M for Murder*

49. David Smith in *Mr. and Mrs. Smith*

50. Iris Henderson in *The Lady Vanishes*

51. Strauss the elder in *Waltzes from Vienna*

52. Jack Sanders in *The Ring*

53. Emily Hill in *Rich and Strange*

54. Shaw Brandon in *Rope*

55. L. B. Jeffries in *Rear Window*

56. Father Michael Logan in *I Confess*

57. Mark Halliday in *Dial M for Murder*

58. Captain Wiles in *The Trouble with Harry*

59. Midge Wood in *Vertigo*

60. Mrs. Brenner in *The Birds*

61. Sarah Sherman in *Torn Curtain*

62. Fran in *Family Plot*

63. Rose Balestrero in *The Wrong Man*

64. Barbara Morton in *Strangers on a Train*

65. Jack Favell in *Rebecca*

66. Beaky in *Suspicion*

67. Milton Arbogast in *Psycho*

68. Babs Milligan in *Frenzy*

69. Philip Vandamm in *North by Northwest*

70. Alexander Sebastian in *Notorious*

71. Abbott in *The Man Who Knew Too Much* (1934)

72. Sam Flusky in *Under Capricorn*

73. Arnie Rogers in *The Trouble with Harry*

74. Caroline in *Psycho*

75. Annie Hayworth in *The Birds*

ACTOR

A. Paul Newman	Q. Cary Grant
B. Peter Lorre	R. Patricia Hitchcock
C. Vera Miles	S. Ingrid Bergman
D. Joan Fontaine	T. Jerry Mathers
E. Henry Fonda	U. Laurence Olivier
F. Karen Black	V. Gregory Peck
G. Sean Connery	W. William Bendix
H. Julie Andrews	X. Charles Laughton
I. Anthony Perkins	Y. Rod Taylor
J. James Stewart	Z. Barbara Bel Geddes
K. Eva Marie Saint	AA. Marlene Dietrich
L. Grace Kelly	BB. Martin Balsam
M. John Dall	CC. Kim Novak
N. Doris Day	DD. Madeleine Carroll
O. Tippi Hedren	EE. Nova Pilbeam
P. Raymond Burr	FF. Barry Foster

GG. Montgomery Clift

HH. Robert Montgomery

II. James Mason

JJ. Joel McCrea

KK. Robert Cummings

LL. Anny Ondra

MM. Carole Lombard

NN. Joan Barry

OO. Jessica Tandy

PP. Nigel Bruce

QQ. Tallulah Bankhead

RR. Leslie Banks

SS. Farley Granger

TT. Edmund Gwenn

UU. George Sanders

VV. Robert Walker

WW. Ray Milland

XX. Anne Baxter

YY. John Forsythe

ZZ. Claude Rains

AAA. Joseph Cotten

BBB. Carl Brisson

CCC. Anna Massey

DDD. Bruce Dern

EEE. Shirley MacLaine

FFF. Margaret Lockwood

GGG. Janet Leigh

HHH. Suzanne Pleshette

QUIZ 9

Offstage:
Facts behind the Filming

Many of the actors who starred in Hitchcock films became immortalized in their roles. However, it may be surprising to learn that some of those players were not Hitchcock's first casting choice. Also, in many instances, the dramatics that occurred backstage between director and actor proved to be as exciting as what appeared on screen. The following quiz contains fifteen true/false statements concerning this topic.

1. Hitchcock vetoed David Niven for the role of Max de Winter in *Rebecca*.

2. The ending of *Suspicion* was reshot after the sneak preview because the suicide scene at the conclusion was a violation of the Production Code.

3. Reflecting upon the failure of *Under Capricorn*, Hitchcock expressed the opinion that Joseph Cotten was not right for the screen lead, and that Laurence Olivier would have been more the type.

4. Gary Cooper turned down the lead in *Foreign Correspondent* because he was under contract with a competing studio.

5. When Hitchcock could not sign William Holden for the role of the tennis pro in *Strangers on a Train*, Farley Granger was hired instead.

6. During the filming of *The Birds* Tippi Hedren suffered a physical and emotional breakdown from juggling a hectic and demanding shooting schedule and the role of being a single parent offstage.

7. Hitchcock was forced to cast Julie Andrews and Paul Newman as leads in the film *Torn Curtain* because the studio wanted the two most popular stars of the day in order to guarantee a success at the box office.

8. Hitchcock tried to sign Liza Minnelli for the role of Blanche in *Family Plot*, but the studio objected.

9. For the female lead role in *North by Northwest*, MGM tried to pressure Hitchcock to cast Cyd Charisse.

10. Anne Baxter was considered for the leading role in *Rebecca*.

11. Hitchcock's first choice to play the key part of David Smith in *Mr. and Mrs. Smith* was Laurence Olivier.

12. The character of Emma in the movie *Shadow of a Doubt* was modeled after Hitchcock's wife, Alma.

13. The original title for the movie *Shadow of a Doubt* was *The Two Charlies*.

14. Alfred Hitchcock's marriage proposal to his wife, Alma, was later written into the script for a scene in the movie *Mr. and Mrs. Smith*.

15. Hitchcock had hoped to cast Cary Grant in the role of the former schoolmaster in *Rope*.

QUIZ **10**

Remakes: Timeless Themes

Hitchcock's masterpieces have been remade into feature films and TV movies, and in celebrating the recent centennial of Hitchcock's birth (1899), a number of his suspense thrillers have been, or are in the process of being, remade. For example, one of the most recent updates, *A Perfect Murder* (1998), is based on Hitchcock's 1954 screen hit *Dial M for Murder*. Producer Arnold Kopelson cast Gwyneth Paltrow as Emily Taylor, the Margot Wendice character played by Grace Kelly in 1954, and Michael Douglas in the role played by Ray Milland in Hitchcock's original film. The following quiz contains ten short-answer questions about Hitchcock remakes and re-releases, as well as films based on his movies.

1. How did the main characters differ in the CBS-TV telefeature *Once You Meet a Stranger* that aired on September 25, 1996, from Hitchcock's 1951 masterpiece *Strangers on a Train?*
   A. They were neighbors.   B. They were women.
   C. They were twins.   D. They were lovers.

2. In the picture, *Dial M for Murder*, Margot Wendice (Grace Kelly) uses a pair of scissors to defend herself against Swan (Anthony Dawson). What does Emily Taylor (Gwyneth Paltrow) use to kill her attacker in the 1998 update, *A Perfect Murder?*
   A. She pushes her attacker down the stairs.
   B. In the struggle, her attacker trips and falls on a fireplace poker.
   C. She stabs her attacker in the throat with a meat thermometer.
   D. She wrestles with her attacker over his gun and shoots him.

3. Which Hitchcock classic thriller, released in late 1998, starring Vince Vaughn and Anne Heche, used the director's original shooting script?
   A. *North by Northwest*   B. *The Birds*
   C. *Marnie*   D. *Psycho*

4. Which Hitchcock thriller that aired on ABC-TV in late 1998 was revamped by producer David Picker, and starred Christopher Reeve?
   A. *Rear Window*   B. *Rope*
   C. *Lifeboat*   D. *The Trouble with Harry*

5. Which Brian de Palma movie released in 1976, starring Cliff Robertson and Genevieve Bujold, was a retelling of Hitchcock's startling 1958 film *Vertigo?*
   A. *Body Double*   B. *Sisters*
   C. *Obsession*   D. *Raising Cain*

6. Which Hitchcock film made in the 1940s was remade twice? The first remake appeared in 1958 under the title *Step Down to Terror*, starring Colleen Miller, Charles Drake, and Rod Taylor. Thirty-three years later, a television movie under the original title was remade.
   A. *Suspicion*   B. *Notorious*
   C. *The Paradine Case*   D. *Shadow of a Doubt*

7. Which 1950s Hollywood movie is Hitchcock's only remake of one of his 1930s British films?

    A. *The 39 Steps*   B. *The Man Who Knew Too Much*

    C. *The Lady Vanishes*   D. *Blackmail*

8. Which Hitchcock drama, restored and re-released in 1996, was a huge commercial success?

    A. *Rear Window*   B. *Vertigo*

    C. *Rope*   D. *I Confess*

9. Which Hitchcock spy picture about a wealthy, young woman being used as a political pawn in a deadly game of love and betrayal, was remade and shown on TV in January 1992?

    A. *Notorious*   B. *Saboteur*

    C. *Foreign Correspondent*   D. *The Secret Agent*

10. Which movie, a tribute loosely based on 1960's *Psycho*, starred Michael Caine in a blond wig?

    A. *Sisters*   B. *Obsession*

    C. *Carrie*   D. *Dressed to Kill*

CHAPTER 2

The 1920s—
cutting the mustard

"I was very happy doing the scripts and the art direction; I hadn't thought of myself as a director."

ALFRED HITCHCOCK, 1967

IN 1925, BRITISH DIRECTOR/PRODUCER MICHAEL BALCON asked Alfred Hitchcock if he would like to try his hand at directing. While content with his then-current position as script writer for Gainsborough Pictures, Hitchcock must have had his eye on the director's chair, because he immediately accepted the challenge and left for Munich to direct his first film (*The Pleasure Garden*). The novice director's style and creative genius were evident from the beginning. Yet the very same artistic technique, which eventually made him a legend, almost ended his career before it began. Hitchcock's initial three films (the second of which, *The Mountain Eagle*, about the hillbillies of Kentucky, has vanished, with no print of it known to exist) were shelved at the behest of financier C. M. Woolf, head of Gainsborough film distribution. Unable to appreciate Hitchcock's filming innovations, Woolf feared that Hitchcock's bizarre style would have negative effects on other pictures produced by the studio. He told Hitchcock directly that the director's third effort, *The Lodger* (1926), was "so dreadful that we're just going to have to put it on the shelf and forget about it."

Nonetheless, Michael Balcon recognized Hitchcock's creativity, and believed in his potential as a filmmaker. Balcon persuaded Ivor Montagu, founder of the Film Society, to modify *The Lodger* and make some improvements. A few awkward scenes were reshot, and the title cards were edited and reduced in number. After a press screening two months later, the film review magazine, *Bioscope*, declared *The Lodger* to be "the finest British production ever made." And according to Donald Spoto in his book, *The Dark Side of Genius: The Life of Alfred Hitchcock* (1983), "It was the first time in British film history that the director received an even greater press than his stars." Later, after the long-awaited release of *The Pleasure Garden*, the London press described Hitchcock as "a young man with a master mind."

The director's chair transformed a shy, quiet script writer into the world's most masterful and best known director. After nine silent films, Hitchcock brought his first decade of filmmaking to a close with *Blackmail* (1929), his first sound picture. The filming had a curious similarity to the plot of a future non-Hitchcock movie, *Singin' in the Rain* (1952) starring Gene Kelly and Debbie Reynolds: the leading lady's voice was too unrefined for the public ear. So, as in the Gene Kelly movie musical, the voice of the female lead (Anny Ondra) in *Blackmail* was dubbed and the picture saved, although the career of Ondra was over. Adding sound to a film was merely a new technical detail and was hardly a problem for Hitchcock. His creative genius was in his visual effects.

QUIZ **11**

The Pleasure Garden

GAINSBOROUGH-EMELKA (1925), B&W, 85 MINUTES

The production of Alfred Hitchcock's first film was completed in London in 1925. Critic Cedric Belfrage, with the British *Picturegoer* wrote, "Hitchcock has such a complete grasp of all the different branches of film technique that he is able to take far more control of his production than the average director of four times his experience." However, due to these same innovative techniques, the studio was concerned that the public would be confused and put off by *The Pleasure Garden*. The silent film was shelved for almost two years before it was released. The following quiz contains five multiple choice questions about this film which almost did not make it out of the studio storeroom.

1. How does Jill manage to get a job dancing at the cabaret?
   A. She answers an ad in the newspaper.
   B. Her friend Patsy arranges for her to work at the theatre.
   C. She catches the eye of the manager, who hires her on the spot.
   D. She auditions and the manager hires her.

2. Why do Hugh and Jill separate after they become engaged?
   A. Hugh is in the service and is transferred.
   B. Hugh travels to Africa to make a quick fortune and believes that life in the wild is too dangerous for Jill.
   C. Jill requests they put some distance between themselves to make sure they have made the right decision.
   D. Hugh wants to travel around the world before getting married.

3. What does Patsy discover when she joins her husband in the tropics?
   A. He is suffering from malaria.
   B. He is living with a native woman.
   C. He forgot that she was coming.
   D. He has amnesia from a riding accident.

4. What is Levett's reaction to Patsy's threat to leave him?
   A. He encourages her to divorce him.
   B. He loses his mind and attempts to kill her.
   C. He starts to regain his memory.
   D. He accuses her of having a lover.

5. Who saves Patsy from her husband's sword?

    A. The brother of Levet's mistress.

    B. Jill, who happened to follow her.

    C. A local doctor.

    D. The houseboy who hates Levet.

QUIZ **12**

The Lodger:
A Story of the London Fog

GAINSBOROUGH (1926), B&W, 125 MINUTES

The Lodger opened on February 14, 1927, in London to rave reviews. Within a few days, ticket buyers formed lines at the cinema that lasted from noon to midnight. With the movie such a hit, Alfred Hitchcock's film career was assured. When *The Lodger* was released in the United States, it was retitled *The Case of Jonathan Drew*. The following quiz contains five short-answer questions about the picture, which is believed to be based on the story of Jack the Ripper.

1. What does the killer use as his calling card?

2. When does the killer commit the murders?

3. When the lodger rents a room from the Buntings, what change does he demand in the decoration of the room?

4. What is in the black bag the lodger kept locked?

5. What circumstance proves the lodger's innocence?

QUIZ **13**

Downhill

GAINSBOROUGH (1927), B&W, 95 MINUTES

Downhill was based on a London drama written by stage and film star Constance Collier and the film's leading man, Ivor Novello, the latter using the pseudonym of David LeStrange. *Downhill*'s theme of devout loyalty between friends appealed to Hitchcock, who used it in at least six other films including *Frenzy*, filmed forty-five years later. (When released in the United States, *Downhill* was retitled *When Boys Leave Home*.) The following quiz contains five true/false statements.

1. The title symbolizes the theme of the downward spiral of society.

2. Roddy takes the blame for fathering his friend's illegitimate child.

3. Dejected, Roddy leaves for America.

4. In order to make a living, Roddy becomes a prize fighter.

5. Roddy returns home to find that his friend has finished school and has become a successful and well-respected businessman.

QUIZ **14**

Easy Virtue

GAINSBOROUGH (1927), B&W, 75 MINUTES

Hitchcock continued to hone his technical skills as a filmmaker. In *Easy Virtue*, he designed life-sized props and used mirrors and doubles for his actors to achieve certain difficult screen images. However, because of the uncertainty of the future of the British film industry and the shakeup of its infrastructure, this was the last picture Hitchcock made for Gainsborough Studios. He soon transferred to British International Pictures. The following quiz contains five multiple choice questions.

1. Where does Larita first encounter John Whittaker?
   A. Larita and John meet on the Mediterranean in the south of France.
   B. Larita and John cross paths in the hallway of the courthouse immediately after her divorce is granted.
   C. Larita and John are introduced to one another on a train to Marseilles.
   D. Larita and John meet in a pub on the afternoon that her divorce is granted.

2. Why does John's family disapprove of Larita?
   A. They know nothing about her.
   B. She is from a different social class.
   C. John and Larita eloped and did not have a traditional Christian wedding.
   D. Because of his marriage to her, John decided not to further his education.

3. How does John's family find out about Larita's scandalous past?
   A. An anonymous envelope arrives containing the newspaper report announcing Larita's divorce.
   B. John's sister finds an old newspaper with the story of Larita's divorce.
   C. John's mother recognizes Larita's name and asks a friend who owns a news-paper to investigate Larita.
   D. Larita's attorney is also the Whittakers' attorney.

4. What is John's reaction when he finds out that Larita is divorced?
   A. John stands up for his wife and decides that his family is unfair and condescending.
   B. John is indifferent to the discovery and chastises his family for overreacting.
   C. John says he knew about Larita's divorce before he married her.
   D. John doubts her love and eventually rejects Larita.

5. What are Larita's famous last words to the photographers as she descends the steps of the courthouse for the second time?
   A. "Take your pictures, they will be the last."
   B. "Remember this face; it is the face of righteous virtue."
   C. "We have done this before."
   D. "Shoot! There's nothing left to kill."

QUIZ **15**

The Ring

BRITISH INTERNATIONAL (1927), B&W, 30 MINUTES

The Ring was Hitchcock's first original screenplay. The deliberate ambiguity reflected in the movie's title, which became prevalent in many later films by the master filmmaker, represents both a boxing ring and a wedding ring. The following quiz contains five short-answer questions.

1. What is symbolic about Jack's winning the fight with Bob Corby?

2. Where is Nellie during Jack's pre-championship fight?

3. What does Nellie use as a shield to protect herself against Jack's rage?

4. What happens in the third round that causes Nellie to realize she still loves her husband?

5. What symbolic phrase does Nellie use to let Jack know she is on his side?

QUIZ 16

The Farmer's Wife

BRITISH INTERNATIONAL (1928), B&W, 156 MINUTES

While filming *The Farmer's Wife* on location in Devon and Surrey, England, Hitchcock had the opportunity to tour the English countryside. Inspired by its serene lifestyle, he suggested to his wife, Alma, that they purchase a house in the country. By the end of the year, the Hitchcocks were proud owners of an estate called Winter's Grace in the village of Shamley Green, thirty miles southwest of London. The following quiz contains five true/false statements.

1. Mrs. Sweetland's last words to Araminta before Mrs. Sweetland died are, "Make sure Samuel finds another wife."

2. The first woman turns down Samuel's proposal of marriage because she does not want to live on a farm and lead the life of a farmer's wife.

3. Samuel brings a basket of plums to his second prospect.

4. The third woman Samuel proposes to laughs and thinks the proposal is a joke because Samuel is too old for her.

5. Samuel suggests marriage to Araminta by handing her Mrs. Sweetland's apron.

Trivia Facts:
Did You Know That . . .

It Was His Blue Period—Hitchcock gave a bizarre dinner party for British stage star Gertrude Lawrence in which he arranged for the food to be dyed blue.

Get It Yourself!—After the filming of *The Farmer's Wife* (1928), Hitchcock invited the cast and crew to celebrate at a West End restaurant. Unbeknownst to his guests, Hitchcock had hired actors to pose as waiters, with instructions to be rude and insulting.

Make Her an Offer She Can't Refuse—Hitchcock proposed marriage to Alma on a stormy night as they crossed the North Sea on their way back to England. She was apparently lying in her cabin queasy with seasickness when he popped the question. Hitchcock later revealed that he felt Alma, in her incapacitated state, would be less likely to reject his proposal.

Not Funny—Hitchcock bet property man Rodney Ackland a week's salary that he could not spend the night alone in the dark, deserted London studio. Besides handcuffing Ackland to the camera, Hitchcock gave him a glass of brandy laced with a strong laxative.

Green Around the Gills—In order to enhance Ivor Novello's delirious state in *Downhill* (1927), Hitchcock requested that the editor tint the film with a pale green color.

American Invasion—Because of the popularity of American films in England, the British film industry was experiencing an economic downward spiral which threatened permanent ruin. To prevent this disaster, the London Council passed the Cinematography Films Act of 1927, binding exhibitors and distributors to running a certain quota of British films annually in their theatres.

Just the Beginning—After working in the film industry for less than seven years, Hitchcock became the highest paid director in England in 1927.

QUIZ **17**

Champagne

BRITISH INTERNATIONAL (1928), B&W, 75 MINUTES

It was a customary economic move for the studio to use the same extras in its films, but Hitchcock demanded "new faces" for the British-made *Champagne*. He instructed his assistant director, Frank Mills, to search cabarets throughout London looking for fresh extras for this silent movie that was ironically reviewed by the critics as "flat." The following quiz contains five multiple choice questions.

1. What is the significance of the title, *Champagne*?
    A. It represents the cavalier lifestyle Betty is leading.
    B. It comes from the fact that Betty's father is in the champagne industry.
    C. It derives from the fact that Betty is reduced to selling champagne in a cabaret.
    D. The movie begins and ends at a cocktail party where everyone is drinking champagne.

2. What message does Betty's father bring her while she is still on the ship?
    A. He will disown her if she marries Jean.
    B. She will have to attend college.
    C. She is cut off financially.
    D. His stock has fallen and they are ruined financially.

3. How does Betty respond when Jean offers to marry her in spite of the situation?
    A. She throws him out because she thinks he pities her.
    B. She wants their situation to improve first.
    C. She becomes angry because she believes he is trying to rescue her.
    D. She refuses his proposal, saying she no longer loves him.

4. Why does Betty run off to America with an older man?

   A. The older gentleman offers to be her friend.

   B. She feels that her life is hopeless and she wants to start afresh in a new country.

   C. She is trying to hurt her father.

   D. She is hoping to escape her memories of Jean.

5. What message does Betty's father give her during this second sea voyage?

   A. He has changed his mind.

   B. His first message to her was a lie.

   C. He wants to forgive her.

   D. He has turned their financial situation around.

QUIZ **18**

The Manxman

BRITISH INTERNATIONAL (1929), B&W, 129 MINUTES

When *The Manxman* was completed in 1928, producer John Maxwell was so disappointed that he shelved the British-made silent film. However, when it was finally released on January 23, 1929, much to Hitchcock's surprise, the press gave *The Manxman* very favorable reviews and the public adored it. The following quiz contains five short-answer questions.

1. Why does Pete go to Africa?

2. What is Kate's first comment when she finds out that Pete has supposedly died?

3. To whom does Kate turn when she leaves Pete?

4. What ultimatum does Kate give Philip?

5. What does Kate do after Pete refuses to give her the baby?

QUIZ **19**

Blackmail

BRITISH INTERNATIONAL (1929), B&W, 86 MINUTES

With the close of the decade, Hitchcock opened a new dimension of film-making, one that earned him praise from some of his toughest critics in London. *Blackmail*, issued in both sound and silent versions, was his first talkie, and critic Hugh Castle had this comment: "It must be said . . . that, considering that he was toying with a medium about which he knew nothing . . . he has made a good job of it. *Blackmail* is perhaps the most intelligent mixture of sound and silence we have yet seen." Castle goes on to characterize *Blackmail* as Hitchcock's comeback after the disappointment of *Champagne* and *The Manxman*. The following quiz contains five true/false statements.

1. When Alice goes to the stranger's apartment, he convinces her to pose nude.

2. Alice stabs and kills the artist because he tries to rape her.

3. The blackmailer uses Alice's glove, which he finds at the scene of the crime, as evidence of her guilt.

4. The word "murder" is uttered several times during breakfast, causing Alice great consternation.

5. Alice visits the chief inspector to confess to the crime.

CHAPTER **3**

The 1930s—
gaining Momentum

"Sequences can never stand still;

they must carry the action forward, just as

the wheels of a ratchet mountain railway move

the train up the slope, cog by cog."

ALFRED HITCHCOCK, 1967

FILM DIRECTING IN THE 1930S WAS A SERIES OF PEAKS and valleys for Alfred Hitchcock. As a "rookie," under contract with British International Pictures, Hitchcock was forced to accept screen assignments that were of little appeal to him. His initial films made in the thirties were adaptations of novels and plays; and the restrictions placed upon him by the studio executives left Hitchcock unenthusiastic and aloof.

The first project that did intrigue Hitchcock was his autobiographical creation, *Rich and Strange* (1932), but, sadly, it turned out to be a commercial failure. After directing two more features (*Number Seventeen*, a confusing thriller attempting to be satirical, and a musical, *Waltzes from Vienna*, which had the double distinction of being just plain dull and the only musical Hitchcock ever directed), he described his career as being at its "lowest ebb." However, the slump was short-lived and his career was resurrected with the creation of the first of four espionage thrillers, *The Man Who Knew Too Much* (1934).

Having regained faith in himself, Hitchcock had yet to convince C. M. Woolf, who was still in charge of distribution for London-based Gainsborough Pictures. Woolf considered all of Hitchcock's films too confusing for the public. He described *The Man Who Knew Too Much* as "utter nonsense," and planned to have it reshot. Producers Michael Balcon and Ivor Montagu came to Hitchcock's rescue again and convinced Woolf to release the film as it was, as the second picture of a double feature. Critics gave the film rave reviews, and Hitchcock's success continued on through 1934 and his next two projects.

However, Hitchcock's popularity took another temporary downturn. The British economy was in dire straits during the 1930s, the Great Depression encompassed the world, and the British film industry was affected by these circumstances. Along with the economic slump in the industry, a subtle, but critical attitude was also developing toward Hitchcock as a true artist. Some established and traditional artists thought Hitchcock's films to be only simple entertainment, and did not recognize them for their artistic quality. The condescending attitude of those in his profession toward him as a director, coupled with being forced to direct films that were not of his choosing, caused Hitchcock to turn his focus on America where his films and talent were held in high regard. In the hope of receiving proper recognition for his work, Hitchcock moved another *cog* in his life forward by selling his home, packing up his family, and moving to America.

QUIZ **20**

Juno and the Paycock

BRITISH INTERNATIONAL (1930), B&W, 95 MINUTES

Alfred and Alma Hitchcock adapted Sean O'Casey's play *Juno and the Paycock* merely as an assignment to fulfill a contract with British International Pictures. Despite their disinterest in the play while shooting the drama, the picture received great reviews. When it was distributed in the United States, the title was changed to *The Shame of Mary Boyle*. The following quiz contains five multiple choice questions.

1. What is Captain Boyle's excuse for not working?
   A. A heart condition
   B. An injured back
   C. Bad legs
   D. Poor blood; work makes him weary

2. What is the apparent good fortune bestowed upon the Boyles?
   A. The Boyles inherit money from a cousin.
   B. Juno, a.k.a. Mrs. Boyle, wins a lottery pool.
   C. Mr. Boyle receives financial compensation for an injury.
   D. Juno is financially compensated after offering assistance to a stranger.

3. What odd, but humorous habit does Joxer, Captain Boyle's neighbor, have?
   A. Joxer often breaks out in song.
   B. Joxer spells his words instead of voicing them, often misspelling them in the process.
   C. Joxer mimes his messages when he gets excited.
   D. Joxer often speaks in verse.

4. What does Juno buy after she purchases new furniture?
   A. A new car
   B. A gramophone and record
   C. A bridal gown for her daughter
   D. A new hat

5. What does Juno decide to do when everything falls apart?
   A. Juno leaves her husband and sends Mary to a convent.
   B. Juno sells the house to pay for the new purchases and to allow Mary to leave town.
   C. Juno throws her husband out and tries to find a job to support herself and Mary.
   D. Juno and Mary go to live with Juno's sister.

QUIZ **21**

Murder!

BRITISH INTERNATIONAL (1930), B&W, 100 MINUTES

To increase ticket sales in Europe, Hitchcock was asked to film a second version of the British-made *Murder* in German. The popular German actor Alfred Abel, who played the lead in this German-language adaptation titled *Mary*, refused to take part in one of the comedy scenes because such frivolity was beneath his dignity. Hitchcock answered the complaining performer by explaining, "The whole point of comedy is to reduce dignity." Abel's response was, "Not for the Germans." The following quiz contains five short-answer questions.

1. For what crime is Diana being tried?

2. Who is convinced of Diana's innocence and conducts a private investigation?

3. What is the original vote from the jury?

4. How does Sir John elicit a confession from the real killer?

5. What two disguises does the real killer use to escape from the scene of the crime?

The Skin Game

BRITISH INTERNATIONAL (1931), B&W, 86 MINUTES

In shooting John Galsworthy's play, *The Skin Game*, Hitchcock rehearsed every scene before filming by acting each role himself for the cast until he was satisfied that the actors understood exactly what he visualized on screen. However, for the suicide sequence where Phyllis Konstam throws herself into a garden pool, he stood on the sidelines, demanding that the actress be flung into the water for ten retakes until he was satisfied that he had captured the perfect shot. The following quiz contains five true/false statements.

1. Mr. Hornblower, the new landowner, wants to cut down the trees in Long Meadows and Century Meadows and build factories.

2. Mr. Hornblower offers to cut Mr. Hillcrist in for 25 percent of any profit if Mr. Hillcrist will help win the neighbors over to Mr. Hornblower's idea.

3. Chloe used to make money by staying with men in hotels in order to give them grounds for divorce.

4. Chloe leaves in the middle of the night when she finds out her secret has been made public.

5. The film ends with a forest fire.

 QUIZ **23**

Rich and Strange

BRITISH INTERNATIONAL (1932), B&W, 83 MINUTES

During the 1920s, Elsie Randolph became one of the most popular stage actresses on London's West End, starring in musicals and comedies. In 1932, she was invited to meet with Hitchcock to discuss the possibility of starring in her first motion picture, as a colorful dowager, a passenger on board the cruise ship *Rich and Strange*. However, because of Randolph's glamour and poise, Hitchcock was doubtful whether she could manage the role of a dowdy, boring old woman. In response to Hitchcock's questions, "How do you feel about this part? Do you think you understand this eccentric character?" Randolph quickly responded by putting on a pair of thick glasses, pulling her hair back and saying in a high-pitched voice, "Oh, well, sir, I've just had my lunch of lark's tongue on toast, and I feel anything is possible!" Randolph was given a supporting role, and within a few weeks Hitchcock and she became close friends. (When later released in the United States, *Rich and Strange* was given the new title of *East of Shanghai*.) The following quiz contains five multiple choice questions.

1. Why does Fred's uncle give Fred and Emily so much money?
   A. He visits their apartment and is appalled at their lack of luxuries.
   B. He wants Fred and Emily to experience life by traveling around the world.
   C. Right before Fred's mother died, he promised to help Fred and Emily.
   D. He is trying to keep from paying so many taxes, and he wants his relatives to have the money instead of the government.

2. How does Emily become acquainted with Commander Gordon?
   A. She meets him on the deck while Fred is in their cabin suffering from seasickness.
   B. She encounters him while playing shuffleboard.
   C. She is introduced to him during a bridge tournament.
   D. He notices that she is dining alone and asks to join her.

3. How does Fred meet the Princess?
   A. She walks into his cabin by mistake.
   B. She pays the bartender to deliver a message to him saying she wants to meet him.
   C. She accidentally hits him in the eye with a puck.
   D. She is chastising her maid for forgetting her cigarettes, and he offers the Princess one of his.

4. What happens to all of Fred and Emily's money?
   A. Fred loses it gambling.
   B. Fred gives it to the Princess.
   C. It is stolen.
   D. Emily gives it to Commander Gordon so he will help her get a divorce.

5. Under what conditions do Fred and Emily make up?
   A. Emily has a breakdown and Fred realizes that he still loves her.
   B. The Princess shoots Fred and he almost dies.
   C. They are afraid that they are going to die when the ship begins to sink.
   D. They are floating in the middle of the ocean in a life raft.

QUIZ **24**

Number Seventeen

BRITISH INTERNATIONAL (1932), B&W, 61 MINUTES

In 1931, Hitchcock had his heart set on directing John Van Druten's play *London Wall*. Instead British International Pictures assigned Hitchcock to film *Number Seventeen*. Ironically, after retitling *London Wall* to *After Office Hours* (1932), the studio gave the project to another contract director, Thomas Bentley, who had actually wanted to film *Number Seventeen*. As retaliation against his studio employer, Hitchcock decided to turn *Number Seventeen* into a subtle satire. Hitchcock, his wife, Alma, and scriptwriter Rodney Ackland developed the scenario at Hitchcock's home where the atmosphere was more jovial than at the studio. When the movie was released, the audience was confused and failed to recognize the humor. The following quiz contains five short-answer questions.

1. Who are the secret agents supposed to meet at Number Seventeen?

2. What humorous event happens every time a gun is fired?

3. Under what circumstances do the young girl and the detective meet?

4. Where is the diamond necklace hidden?

5. Who ends up with the necklace?

QUIZ **25**

The Man Who Knew Too Much

GAUMONT-BRITISH (1934), B&W, 110 MINUTES

Hitchcock conceived the idea for this film while he and Alma were on their honeymoon in St. Moritz in 1926. Awed by the beauty and style of this luxury Swiss resort, Hitchcock began to imagine what would happen if a carefree family's vacation came to an abrupt halt by the kidnapping of their child by foreign secret agents. Eight years later, this fantasy became a reality as Hitchcock prepared for the filming of *The Man Who Knew Too Much*, which was set, of course, in St. Moritz. The following quiz contains six multiple choice questions.

1. What contest does Jill Lawrence lose during her stay at the ski resort?
   A. Bridge
   B. Skeet shooting
   C. Cross-country skiing
   D. Bobsledding

2. What tragedy occurs when Louis Bernard and Jill are dancing?
   A. A sniper shoots and kills Bernard.
   B. Bob and Jill's daughter is kidnapped.
   C. An avalanche kills a team of cross-country skiers.
   D. The local police raid the resort looking for spies.

3. Where does Louis tell Jill to find the secret message that is hidden in his room?
   A. Behind a loose tile in the shower
   B. In the light fixture
   C. Taped onto the top shelf of the medicine cabinet
   D. Hidden in a shaving brush

4. What message do the kidnappers deliver to Mr. Lawrence?
    A. "Keep your wife quiet or we will silence your entire family."
    B. "Children and wives should be seen and not heard."
    C. "Say nothing of what you found or you will never see your child again."
    D. "We will keep your child long enough to make sure you keep quiet."

5. What secret does Bob and Jill learn from Louis Bernard?
    A. A foreign diplomat in London is to be assassinated.
    B. The prime minister of Great Britain is to be kidnapped.
    C. Windsor Castle is to be bombed.
    D. Several historical sites in London are to be sabotaged.

6. Who saves Betty from her kidnappers and how?
    A. Bob chases one of the kidnappers, causing him to fall off the roof of the church.
    B. Nurse Agnes helps Betty escape down the fire escape.
    C. Mrs. Lawrence shoots Betty's pursuer as he chases her across the roof.
    D. Clive disguises Betty as a nun and ushers her out of the church.

QUIZ

The 39 Steps

GAUMONT-BRITISH (1935), B&W, 81 MINUTES

During the filming of *The 39 Steps*, writer Angus MacPhail coined the term "MacGuffin," which Hitchcock continued to use throughout his movie-making career. The term referred to an insignificant event that simply jump-started the story. The concept developed after MacPhail told the story about two men traveling from London to Scotland by train. One traveler inquired about a curious package in the luggage rack. The conversation went as follows:

"What have you there?" asked one of the men.

"Oh, that's a MacGuffin," replied the other.

"What's a MacGuffin?"

"It's a device for trapping lions in the Scottish Highlands."

"But there aren't any lions in the Scottish Highlands!"

"Well, then, I guess that's no MacGuffin!"

The following quiz contains six true/false statements.

1. The stage name for the quiz master is "Mr. Genius."

2. The leader of the spy ring is missing his right earlobe.

3. The bullet lodges in the cigarette case in Richard Hannay's breast pocket, saving his life.

4. Richard and Pamela are forced to stay together after they escape from the police because they are handcuffed together.

5. Pamela and Richard evade the police by hiding in a haystack.

6. The film begins and ends in a train station.

QUIZ **27**

Secret Agent

GAUMONT-BRITISH (1936), B&W, 95 MINUTES

On the set, disputes between the actors and the film's director led to Hitchcock's loss of interest in this project. Hitchcock signed John Gielgud for the male lead because of his stage experience as Shakespeare's *Hamlet*. Hitchcock considered Gielgud's role as a Hamlet-type character, and was hopeful that the actor could add elegance and dimension to the pivotal screen role. However, Gielgud was overworked (as he was concurrently playing in a stage production of *Romeo and Juliet*) and had yet to gain his self-confidence as a movie actor. As a result, he was not at his best, and the distressed Hitchcock focused all of his attention on his leading lady, blonde Madeleine Carroll, ignoring his other performers. To make matters worse, Peter Lorre, who was assigned the role of the notorious general, was disappearing frequently from the sound stage to take care of his morphine addiction. The following quiz contains six short-answer questions.

1. In what dismal location does the film open?

2. What is Edgar Brodie's alias?

3. What did Edgar Brodie do for a living before being recruited to join the war effort?

4. What role does Elsa Carrington play in the operation?

5. What leads Edgar Brodie to believe Mr. Caypor is the German agent?

6. Who really is the German agent?

QUIZ **28**

Sabotage

GAUMONT-BRITISH (1936), B&W, 77 MINUTES

In retrospect, Hitchcock admitted to making a "grave error" when he decided to cast a young boy as the victim of the bomb explosion in this thriller's key scene. Hitchcock felt that the audience developed an emotional attachment to the young character and subsequently became resentful at the child's demise. (When this thriller was shown in the United States, it was renamed *The Woman Alone.*) The following quiz contains six multiple choice questions.

1. What two businesses are used as fronts for the spy ring?
   A. A laundry and a liquor store
   B. A grocery store and a travel agency
   C. A theatre and a pet shop
   D. A magazine stand and a bookstore

2. What is the message Verloc receives from the saboteurs?
   A. LONDON WILL NOT BE HAPPY IN THE MORNING.
   B. LONDON MUST NOT LAUGH ON SATURDAY.
   C. LONDON WILL WAKE UP TO A SURPRISE.
   D. LONDON WILL PAY.

3. How does the saboteur deliver the bomb to Verloc and what is the message that accompanies it?
   A. It is delivered in a grocery box with the message, "Groceries for apartment 145."
   B. It is concealed in a gift parcel with the message, "Don't open until 1:45."
   C. It arrives in a King James Bible with the message, "John 1:45."
   D. It is delivered in a bird cage with the message, "Don't forget—the birds will sing at 1:45."

4. Why does Stevie not reach his destination on time?
   A. He stops to eat buttered scones.
   B. He stops to play ball with a friend.
   C. He is distracted by a street hawker and a parade.
   D. He stops to take a turn around the park on his friend's bicycle.

5. Which Disney film is shown in Verloc's theatre?
   A. *Who Killed Cock Robin?*   B. *The Spider and the Fly*
   C. *The Tortoise and the Hare*   D. *Old King Cole*

6. Which holiday is scheduled to become London's doomsday?
   A. Summer Bank Holiday   B. Guy Fawkes Day
   C. Boxing Day   D. Lord Mayor's Show Day

Trivia Facts:
Did You Know That . . .

Just Whistle a Happy Tune—To entertain his guests at cocktail parties, Hitchcock, on occasion, would paint a sailor's face on his belly, its lips in the shape of an "O" around his navel. He would then whistle a tune while shaking his belly and making it appear as if the painted sailor was whistling.

Come As You Are—Distinguished actor Sir Gerald du Maurier was often the victim of Hitchcock's pranks and practical jokes. On one occasion Hitchcock told Sir Gerald that he was giving a costume party and to dress appropriately. The unsuspecting actor arrived in costume only to discover that the affair was black tie. Sir Gerald fled the party in embarrassment.

A Final Chore—Hitchcock's last work at British International Pictures was to produce *Lord Camber's Ladies* (1932), an overwrought "quota quickie" directed by Benn W. Levy and starring Gertrude Lawrence and Sir Gerald du Maurier.

Speak No Evil—As an act of rebellion toward Elstree Studio for forcing him to direct a thriller, *Number Seventeen* (1932), Hitchcock arranged for one of the heroines to utter not a single word until the very end. His reasoning was that heroines of thrillers were usually "dumb."

What Better Way to Get Acquainted—In *The 39 Steps* (1935), the leading man and lady were handcuffed together for several hours (Hitchcock falsely claiming he had lost the key to the handcuffs) in preparation for a particular scene.

They Don't Even Have a Statue of Liberty—The Brazilian government banned the film *Sabotage* (1936), because they considered it a threat to public order and an invitation to terrorism.

No Smoking Section, Please—While filming *Rich and Strange* (1932) actress Elsie Randolph told Hitchcock that she detested cigarette smoke. Hitchcock, a smoker himself, decided to make Randolph a victim of one of his practical jokes. Randolph was told to sit in a phone booth so that Hitchcock could shoot an extra scene. He then arranged for smoke to be piped into the booth, bringing the young actress to near collapse.

If the Suit Fits—German emigrant actor Peter Lorre and Hitchcock often tried to outdo one another in practical jokes on the sound stage. In one such incident, Hitchcock claimed that Lorre was acting childishly when he complained that the studio had ruined one of his suits. In response to Lorre's complaint, Hitchcock sent Lorre an identical suit tailored to fit an infant.

No Mercy—Teetotaler Mary Clare, the actress who played in *Young and Innocent* (1937) and *The Lady Vanishes* (1938), received an alcohol-laced fruit drink from Hitchcock when he found out about her abstinence.

Silhouette in Christmas—The famous Hitchcock profile sketch, later used in the 1950s and 1960s as part of the introduction to his American television program, originated from a Christmas card he designed while still living in England.

Just Making a Good Impression—In the early days of filmmaking, when Hitchcock lived on Cromwell Road in London, he would often wear a black bathrobe and top hat when interviewing new writers.

QUIZ **29**

Young and Innocent

GAUMONT-BRITISH (1937), B&W, 84 MINUTES

At the completion of *Young and Innocent* in England, negotiations with Selznick International Studio in California had already begun for Hitchcock's possible relocation to the United States. The famous British director was eager to move to America where he believed he would receive the professional recognition he deserved. John Hay Whitney, chairman of Selznick International, and Kay Brown, David O. Selznick's New York representative, viewed *Young and Innocent* (retitled *The Girl Was Young* for U.S. distribution) at a private screening. Whitney was disappointed in the offering and urged Selznick to cease negotiations with Hitchcock. However, Ms. Brown disagreed and convinced Selznick that Hitchcock could, in fact, live up to his famous name and reputation. The following quiz contains six true/false statements.

1. Robert is accused of murdering the actress, Christine Clay, because he was seen running from the body.

2. Robert is an actor.

3. Robert and Christine were married for two months, separated, and then divorced five years later.

4. Robert's motive for murdering Christine is the fact that she left him a sizable amount of money in her will.

5. The police know Robert is hiding in the mill because Robert throws a napkin out of the window.

6. Will recognizes the murderer by the jagged scar under his left eye.

QUIZ **30**

The Lady Vanishes

GAUMONT-BRITISH (1938), B&W, 96 MINUTES

In one of many conversations with French filmmaker François Truffaut over the years, Hitchcock revealed that his interest in the story told in The *Lady Vanishes* grew from a tale revolving around the great Paris exposition of 1880. A mother and daughter traveled to Paris, where the mother became ill. She was attended by a doctor who sent her across the city for medication. When the daughter went to find her mother, the hotel room had been rearranged and the manager denied ever having seen her. Rumor had it that the woman had the bubonic plague and her disappearance was arranged to prevent a panic that was sure to keep tourists away from Paris. The following quiz contains six short-answer questions.

1. How do Iris and Miss Froy meet?

2. Why is Iris disoriented when she boards the train?

3. How does Miss Froy introduce herself to Iris when they are on the train?

4. When does Gilbert realize that Iris is telling the truth about Miss Froy?

5. Before Miss Froy escapes from the train during the ambush, how does she give Gilbert the secret message to deliver to the authorities?

6. When Gilbert forgets the melody, who plays it for him on the piano?

QUIZ **31**

Jamaica Inn

ERICH POMMER/MAYFLOWER (1939), B&W, 99 MINUTES

During the making of *Jamaica Inn*, power struggles developed between Hitchcock and the film's veteran star, Charles Laughton. To get into character, methodical actor Laughton often held up filming inordinately long while he developed an inner feel for a particular scene. For example, on one occasion Laughton asked Hitchcock to film him only in closeup shots because he had not yet perfected the correct walk for his character. Several days later, Laughton announced he had discovered his alter ego's step by whistling a German waltz. The following quiz contains six multiple choice questions.

1. Why are there so many shipwrecks on the Cornish coast of England?
    A. The smugglers use a lantern to simulate a lighthouse and lure the ships into hazardous waters.
    B. The smugglers send distress signals, causing the ships to change course.
    C. The smugglers cover the beacon, causing the ships to wreck on the rocky shores.
    D. The smugglers dynamite the cliffs, causing an avalanche of rocks to fall into the shallow water.

2. Why does Mary come to the Jamaica Inn?
    A. She is seeking a job as a cook.
    B. Her mother died and she is coming to live with her aunt.
    C. She comes to the Jamaica Inn to research her heritage.
    D. Jamaica Inn is her first stop on a journey to escape her abusive husband.

3. How does Mary save Jem, the man the smugglers were about to hang?
   A. She creates a diversion by lighting a fire in the brush behind the house.
   B. She fires three shots through the window.
   C. She reaches through a hole in the floor of her second story room and cuts the rope which is attached to the rafters and to Jim's neck.
   D. She quickly pushes a table under his feet.

4. Who is Jem Traherne?
   A. He is an investigator for Scotland Yard.
   B. He is an officer of the Royal Navy sent to investigate the ship-wrecks.
   C. He works for the coast guard.
   D. He is hired by a shipping merchant's association to investigate the wrecks.

5. Who warns Joss Merlyn that he is about to be captured and hanged?
   A. Mary   B. Jem
   C. Salvation   D. Patience

6. Who is the mastermind behind the smuggling operation?
   A. Patience   B. Joss Merlyn
   C. Sir Humphrey   D. Jem

CHAPTER 4

The 1940s—
The Move to America

"Outside of England, there is a much more universal concept of life, which one gets by talking with people and even by the manner in which they tell a story."

ALFRED HITCHCOCK, 1939

A MERICA IN THE 1940S OFFERED NEW CHALLENGES for the forty-one-year-old Alfred Hitchcock, not all of which he welcomed. He signed with the studio of David O. Selznick, former executive producer for MGM. Their first venture, *Rebecca*, was a resounding success. This film adaptation of Daphne du Maurier's 1938 best-selling novel was nominated for several Academy Awards in 1941. However, the relationship between Selznick and Hitchcock grew tense as their personalities clashed. In this period, Selznick was also preoccupied with the release and promotion of his blockbuster film *Gone With the Wind* (1939). Having little time to deal with his new, temperamental director, and needing to generate cash flow, Selznick ultimately "loaned" Hitchcock to several other American production companies—Wanger Productions, Twentieth Century-Fox, and Universal, to name a few. Working with these companies, Hitchcock directed his usual type of suspense film, but also had the opportunity to experiment with American-style romantic comedy and melodrama.

Although Hitchcock continued to work occasionally with Selznick, the creative freedom given to Hitchcock in these instances did not make up for his disgruntlement with his salary (although it was higher than it had ever been) and with Selznick's interference. Feeling a bit homesick and extremely guilty at having left his mother and country, as Europe was on the verge of war, Hitchcock eventually returned to England in 1944 to direct two propaganda films for the war effort.

Hitchcock also had an ulterior motive for his return. Unbeknownst to Selznick, Hitchcock was collaborating with Sidney Bernstein in London to form a new production company, Transatlantic Pictures, to make movies in America and England. With this enterprise, Hitchcock hoped eventually to marry the innovation of Hollywood with the sophistication of London. Hitchcock and Bernstein produced two fairly successful pictures, (*Rope,* 1948, and *Under Capricorn,* 1949), but the production company was laden with misfortune and they were forced to dissolve their venture.

Alfred Hitchcock ended the decade in the employ of Warner Bros., which distributed *Stage Fright* in 1950. However, its completion left him with no screen project on the horizon. Although Hitchcock's artistic outlook definitely had expanded with his relocation to America, the personal emotional problems he faced in England had followed him across the Atlantic Ocean.

QUIZ **32**

Rebecca

SELZNICK STUDIO/RKO (1940), B&W, 130 MINUTES

In preparing the treatment for his first American-made movie, *Rebecca,* Hitchcock wrote more than one hundred precise, detailed incidents, indicating specific dialogue and camera placement. The confident Hitchcock expected producer David O. Selznick's immediate approval. Instead, Hitchcock received a lengthy critique which began with the comments, "shocked and disappointed beyond words." Years later when Hitchcock was asked about Selznick's memo, the filmmaker responded, "It was so long that I've just now finished reading it. I think it'd made a very good film. I'd call it *The Longest Story Ever Told.*" The following quiz contains ten multiple choice questions.

1. Where do Maxim and the future Mrs. de Winter meet?
   A. At a dinner party   B. On the beach in France
   C. Riding horses in the park D. At a hotel in Monte Carlo

2. What ominous sign greets the newlyweds as they proceed up the drive on the way to Manderley?
   A. There is a full moon rising over the ocean behind the mansion.
   B. The weather turns foul, and it begins to rain.
   C. As soon as they turn off the road onto the driveway, their car breaks down.
   D. Mrs. de Winter is so nervous, she becomes ill.

3. What makes Rebecca's room unique compared to any other room in the house?
   A. Rebecca decorated it herself using a modern motif.
   B. It has a private entrance to the garden.
   C. There is a trap door behind the bookcase.
   D. It is the only one in the house that faces the sea.

4. How does Maxim's new wife discover the cottage in the cove?
   A. She sees the cove from Maxim's bedroom window.
   B. She follows the dog to the cottage.
   C. She stumbles upon it when she is looking for Maxim after an argument.
   D. Mrs. Danvers suggests she take a walk along the trail that leads to the cottage.

5. Why is Maxim angry with his wife's choice of costume on the night of the ball?
   A. It is not the one he had picked out for her to wear.
   B. It is the same costume Rebecca wore to the ball before she died.
   C. It is not a period costume, which breaks with tradition.
   D. She is unknowingly wearing Rebecca's wedding dress.

6. How does Mrs. de Winter choose that particular outfit?
   A. She finds the costume hanging in her closet and assumes Maxim put it there for her to wear.
   B. The costume is delivered to her in a gift box with a note from Maxim's sister saying that it is her brother's favorite.
   C. She finds out what Maxim's costume is and decides that hers would be a good match.
   D. Mrs. Danvers suggests that she wear the costume because it is Maxim's favorite.

7. When Maxim confronted Rebecca in the cottage on the night of her death, what did she tell him that caused him to lose his temper and strike her?
   A. She was leaving him for her lover, and she hoped the scandal would ruin him socially.
   B. She was pregnant with another man's child and Manderley would not be inherited by another de Winter.
   C. She married him for his money and planned to party to her heart's content, taking as many lovers as she pleased.
   D. She knew of a secret that would ruin him, and she planned to blackmail him.

8. What evidence is revealed at the inquest that indicated that Rebecca could have been murdered?
   A. A boat builder testifies that the seacocks on her boat were opened, indicating that the boat had been intentionally sunk.
   B. A doctor testifies that there were bruises on her neck, indicating strangulation.

C. Rebecca was inside the cabin and the door was locked from the outside.

D. A doctor testifies that Rebecca's wounds could not have been self-inflicted.

9. Who tells the authorities that Rebecca had been to a doctor in London?

A. Jack Favell, Rebecca's lover   B. Mrs. Danvers

C. Maxim   D. Maxim's business associate

10. What information supports the theory that Rebecca committed suicide?

A. The authorities found a suicide note.

B. It was initially believed that the cabin door was locked from the inside.

C. Rebecca was dying and had only a short while to live.

D. Mrs. Danvers testifies that Rebecca was depressed and spoke of suicide.

QUIZ 33

Foreign Correspondent

WANGER/UNITED ARTISTS (1940), B&W, 120 MINUTES

In addition to making his now-traditional cameo appearances in his films, Hitchcock included a replication of his own marriage proposal to his future wife, Alma, in the script for *Foreign Correspondent*. The scene occurs on a ship in the stormy North Sea. Johnny Jones (Joel McCrea) proclaims his love for Carol Fisher (Laraine Day), and suggests that they marry. When she quickly accepts, his response is, "Hmmm . . . That cuts down our love scene quite a bit, doesn't it? . . . How do you think your father will feel?" Unlike the romantic scene in the thriller, Alma accepted Hitchcock's proposal between groans and burps due to her seasickness. The following quiz contains eight short-answer questions.

1. What new name does Jones' editor give him for his fresh assignment?

2. Who is the head of the Peace Party in London?

3. How is the assassination attempt on Mr. Van Meer carried out?

4. What does John keep losing during the movie?

5. Who does Mr. Fisher turn out to be?

6. What is the first attempt on John's life?

7. What is the second attempt?

8. How does John surreptitiously get his story to his editor?

QUIZ 34

Mr. and Mrs. Smith

RKO (1941), B&W, 93 MINUTES

Alfred Hitchcock was anxious to begin working on this comedy because his close friend, movie star Carole Lombard, had accepted the female lead. Always eager to outdo Hitchcock in the arena of practical jokes, Lombard arranged for a corral containing three cows to be set up on the sound stage for the first day of shooting, because Hitchcock had recently made the comment that actors were like cattle. The light-hearted banter that occurred off screen between Hitchcock and Lombard was mirrored on the screen between Lombard and her celluloid husband, Robert Montgomery. The following quiz contains five true/false statements.

1. David and Ann Smith barricade themselves in their apartment until David gives in to Ann's wishes.

2. A county official tells David that, due to a civil technicality, he and Ann are not legally married.

3. David moves in with his brother after Ann throws him out of their apartment.

4. Ann tries to make David jealous by announcing her engagement to Jeff, David's business partner.

5. Ann and Jeff go to the Catskills for the weekend to ski.

QUIZ **35**

Suspicion

RKO (1941), B&W, 99 MINUTES

There was much trepidation on the sound stage during the filming of *Suspicion* because Hitchcock had not yet decided on a proper ending to this thriller. After considerable debate, it was determined that Lina McLaidlaw (Joan Fontaine) would be driven to suicide because of her emotional instability and the fact that she has been having an affair. At the sneak preview the audience laughed at this contrived, unbelievable ending. Hitchcock's wife, Alma, and scriptwriter Joan Harrison rewrote the finale, adding a surprising plot twist. When the revamped film was released, the public loved it; however, many critics felt that the climax was still contrived. The following quiz contains eight multiple choice questions.

1. What book is Lina reading when she meets Johnny? Hint: the book may symbolize their forthcoming relationship.
   A. A murder mystery
   B. A book about criminal psychosis
   C. A book about child psychology
   D. A biography of Henry VIII

2. What occurrence causes Lina to defy her parents and her own sense of self and pursue the playboy, Johnny?

   A. Her mother plans to fix her up with a man she hates.

   B. Her father complains about how all of her friends are married or engaged and she is still not dating.

   C. She overhears her father saying that she is acting like a nun.

   D. She overhears her parents discussing her grim future as a spinster.

3. What is Johnny's nickname for Lina?

   A. Monkey face   B. Little rich girl

   C. Philly   D. Miss Freud

4. What gift does Lina's father give Johnny and Lina for their wedding?

   A. A townhouse

   B. A portrait of himself to hang over the fireplace

   C. Lina's father pays for their honeymoon.

   D. Two museum-piece chairs

5. Where does Johnny get the £2,000 that allows him to purchase the extravagant gifts he brings home for Lina?

   A. He borrows the money from an associate.

   B. He steals the money from his employer.

   C. He wins the money at the race track.

   D. He cashes in his insurance policy.

6. What word does Lina spell out in playing anagrams?

   A. Murder   B. Suspicion

   C. Liar   D. Poison

7. What type of business venture are Johnny and Beaky developing?

   A. They are planning to produce a movie.

   B. They intend to buy a racehorse and charge stud fees.

   C. They are negotiating a real estate development venture.

   D. They are planning on going into the import/export business.

8. What does Lina's father leave her in his will?

   A. Nothing

   B. His horse and tack

   C. A yearly inheritance of £500 and his portrait

   D. His entire library

QUIZ **36**

Saboteur

UNIVERSAL (1942), B&W, 77 MINUTES

By 1942, Hitchcock had made four feature films since his relocation to Hollywood. Tension between the temperamental director and producer David O. Selznick came to a climax during the negotiations for *Saboteur*. Hitchcock asked for a bonus prior to working on the script as compensation for being on loan to yet another studio. When Selznick denied the request, Hitchcock stormed out of his office and refused to begin work. Still under a loanout contract with Universal, Hitchcock reluctantly returned to start the film. However, the quality of the finished *Saboteur* was not up to Hitchcock's usual standard. Many people believed Hitchcock's feeling exploited was the reason for the project's inferiority. The following quiz contains eight short-answer questions.

1. How does Barry Kane first come into contact with Fry?

2. Why is Barry running from the police?

3. What is the highway number that is Barry's escape route?

4. How does Barry come to realize that Mr. Tobin is lying about his connection to the terrorist group?

5. How do Barry and Pat meet?

6. Among the circus characters, who casts the deciding vote as to whether to turn Barry and Pat over to the police or to allow them to escape?

7. What is to be sabotaged in the Brooklyn navy yard?

8. How does Pat attempt to call for help when she is held prisoner in the skyscraper?

QUIZ 37

Shadow of a Doubt

UNIVERSAL (1943), B&W, 108 MINUTES

Of all fifty-three Hitchcock feature films, *Shadow of a Doubt* is considered to be the director's most autobiographical. Just as Hitchcock was about to begin working on the script, he received word that his mother was critically ill back in England. Leaving the responsibility for her care solely to his brother, Hitchcock remained in California working under a hectic schedule placed upon him by producer David O. Selznick. Faced with the impending death of his mother, Hitchcock began reflecting on his youth and subsequently put his heart and soul into this project. Before the release of *Shadow of a Doubt*, Hitchcock's feelings of guilt and sadness increased with the shocking news that his fifty-two-year-old brother had apparently committed suicide a few weeks after burying their mother. If there was a bright side to these tragedies, it was Hitchcock's decision to lose 100 pounds (weighing almost 300 pounds, he was having difficulty tying his shoes), so that he would not follow his mother and brother to an early grave. The following quiz contains ten true/false statements.

1. Charlie Oakley is living in a boarding house in room number thirteen.

2. Charlie brings his namesake niece, Charlie, a diamond bracelet.

3. Charlie is suspicious of her gift because of its obvious wear.

4. Joe Newton and his friend like to read and discuss crime novels and murder mysteries.

5. In order to keep the family from reading a certain article in the newspaper, Charlie Oakley pretends to accidentally drop a cigar on the paper, burning a hole in the middle of it.

6. The two investigators, Mr. Graham and Mr. Saunders, pretend to be taking a survey when they go to interview the Newton family concerning Charlie Oakley.

7. Uncle Charlie hides $40,000 in a cigar box in the garage.

8. In spite of the recent development that apparently clears Uncle Charlie as a suspect, his niece, Charlie, still believes that her uncle is guilty of the murders.

9. The melody that Charlie Oakley hums throughout the film is from "The Merry Widow."

10. Charlie Oakley is finally arrested for the murders of the women from the East.

Trivia Facts:
Did You Know That . . .

Yeah, Right!—Tallulah Bankhead refused to wear underwear on the set for the filming of *Lifeboat* (1944) due to the wet conditions (at least that's what she claimed). Her immodesty almost cost the studio major publicity with the *Ladies' Home Journal*, whose reporters were invited on the set.

I Hate It When That Happens—During the filming of *Spellbound* (1945), when he became irritated with David O. Selznick's interference Hitchcock would stop the camera, claiming that it was broken. As soon as the producer left the set, Hitchcock would resume filming.

Trapped in a Nightmare—Famed surrealist artist, Salvador Dali, designed the vivid dream scene in the film *Spellbound*. Dali went overboard in his attempt to capture the full spectrum of Hitchcock's imagination on the screen. Even Hitchcock admitted that Dali's ideas were too bizarre as seen on camera. As a result, much of Dali's creation ended up on the cutting room floor.

You Scratch My Back . . . —In 1949, Hitchcock signed a multi-picture contract with Warner Bros., giving him control of almost every aspect of his films. Wanting to prove himself capable of producing a film that would be more profitable than *Rope* (1948) and *Under Capricorn* (1949), Hitchcock cast Jane Wyman in *Stage Fright*. She had just received the Oscar for Best Actress that year for *Johnny Belinda*. Wyman was eager to begin working right way, because she had just been through a bitter divorce with actor Ronald Reagan.

Shy, Quiet, and Unimposing—In 1946, Hitchcock appeared as a mystery guest on Milton Berle's *Which Is Which* radio show. Hitchcock requested a fee of $4,000, but was paid only half that amount. However, he stumped the studio audience by submitting only the vaguest of biographies and, therefore, won an additional $1,000.

Same Strategy, New Genre—On January 20, 1941, Hitchcock's American-style comedy, *Mr. and Mrs. Smith*, opened at Radio City Music Hall in New York and sold out for the first nine days.

The Scent of a Psychopath?—A special perfume, *Spellbound*, had been created and distributed in 1945 to coincide with the release of Hitchcock's movie of the same name.

Murder by Any Other Name . . .—After a brief run, Hitchcock pulled *Rope* from distribution, stating that he no longer wished it shown. The film's technical achievements were overshadowed by the story content, which by social standards of the times was not acceptable and was even condemned by some educational organizations.

QUIZ 38

Lifeboat

TWENTIETH CENTURY-FOX (1944), B&W, 96 MINUTES

The filming of *Lifeboat* was arduous for the actors in spite of the single confined set—a lifeboat. Hitchcock designed wind fans and water-spraying machines to simulate a stormy sea. The cast was subjected to hours of filming in wet clothes. Many actors became ill, including star Tallulah Bankhead who developed pneumonia. To show his appreciation for such dedication, Hitchcock gave her a Sealyham puppy as a present on the last day of the hectic shooting. Upon presenting the gift, Hitchcock informed his star that he had already named the dog "Hitchcock." The following quiz contains ten short-answer questions.

1. What magazine is floating in the water among the debris?

2. Who says the prayer as they bury the baby at sea?

3. What are each of the passengers' assigned jobs?

4. What does Kovak use to make a deck of cards?

5. How many tattoos does Kovak have?

6. Who does the German crew member turn out to be?

7. Why does Gus jump overboard?

8. What do Connie and Kovak have in common?

9. How is Willi able to stay alert and row the boat for so long?

10. What does Connie suggest they use as fish bait?

QUIZ **39**

Spellbound

SELZNICK INTERNATIONAL/UNITED ARTISTS (1945), B&W, 111 MINUTES

In keeping with his philosophy that actors play but a minor role in the overall success of a film, Hitchcock had a simple solution to Ingrid Bergman's complaints concerning a difficult and uncomfortable scene in *Spellbound* where she was required to remain very still during the shooting. "Fake it," advised Hitchcock. Several years later, Bergman recollected that Hitchcock's advice served her well on several occasions when she found a director's request almost impossible to perform. The following quiz contains eight multiple choice questions.

1. What is the name of the mental hospital where Dr. Constance Petersen works?
   A. Shady Grove   B. Green Manors
   C. Gabriel Valley   D. Springfield Residence

2. What is the name of the book written by Dr. Edwardes?
   A. *Psychosis of the Abnormal Mind*
   B. *Theories of Amnesia and Possible Cures*
   C. *The Labyrinth of the Guilt Complex*
   D. *Hypnosis: The Answer to Neurosis*

3. What visual pattern causes John Ballantine to become hysterical?
   A. A red and black checkerboard
   B. Diamond patterns, as on a harlequin figure
   C. Polka dots
   D. Dark parallel lines on a white background

4. When does Constance realize that John is not Dr. Edwardes?

   A. She finds a picture of Dr. Edwardes on the book jacket of another book authored by him.

   B. She notices that the signature on John's note does not match the signature in Dr. Edwardes' book.

   C. When John cannot answer an academic question, she becomes suspicious.

   D. Her colleague tells her that Dr. Edwardes had a scar on his left ear; John does not have this scar.

5. How does Dr. Brulov manage to sedate John when he comes downstairs with a razor in his hand?

   A. Dr. Brulov swiftly injects John with a sedative while Constance distracts him.

   B. Dr. Brulov places a drug in John's milk.

   C. Dr. Brulov hypnotizes John and he surrenders the razor willingly.

   D. Constance pretends to faint while Dr. Brulov places a chloroform-soaked handkerchief to John's mouth and nose.

6. What trauma eventually led to John's breakdown?

   A. John accidentally killed his brother.

   B. John crawled out onto the ledge of his second story bedroom window to retrieve a kite. He experienced vertigo and fell.

   C. John slipped off a chair lift at a ski resort, but managed to hang on until the lift reached the top.

   D. John almost drowned after falling through the broken ice while skating.

7. Once John regains his memory, what does he recall about what has happened to Dr. Edwardes?

   A. John says that Dr. Edwardes suddenly left the lodge because of an emergency call from his hospital.

   B. John says that Dr. Edwardes felt ill and left for the hospital.

   C. John says that Dr. Edwardes was skiing behind John and never made it down the slope.

   D. John says that Dr. Edwardes had a fatal accident while they were skiing.

8. How does Constance realize the identity of the real murderer?

A. Constance analyzes John's bizarre dream.

B. The murderer states a fact that only a guilty person could have known.

C. Constance glances at some papers on John's desk and is able to put two and two together.

D. Constance remembers something that was said in an earlier conversation.

QUIZ **40**

Notorious

RKO (1946), B&W, 101 MINUTES

Notorious is the engrossing narrative of a passionate love triangle set amid intrigue and espionage in post–World War II South America. Critics consider this entry one of Hitchcock's most tasteful love stories. For years Hitchcock had been fascinated with filming a prolonged kissing scene. However, because of Hollywood's then strict censorship regulations against this display of onscreen passion, he had not, until the mid-1940s, conceived of a way around the restrictions. Hitchcock carefully choreographed the romantic three-minute oncamera scene where Cary Grant and Ingrid Bergman embrace and kiss while talking about food. Evidently, the culinary topic of conversation during the love scene made this display of emotion less lustful to the censors. However, this scene has been regarded as one of the most sensuous in all of Hitchcock's films. A very similar sequence was also filmed in *To Catch a Thief* (1955). The following quiz contains eight true/false statements.

1. It is arranged that Alicia and Alexander are to meet at a cocktail party at the American Embassy.

2. Alicia decides to take her espionage duties one step further and marry Alexander because she finds out that Devlin is already married.

3. Alicia takes the key to the wine cellar when Alexander is changing for a party.

4. Alicia passes the key to Devlin when she hands him his martini.

5. The metal in the wine bottle is plutonium.

6. When Alicia arrives the last time to report to Devlin he believes that her haggard appearance is due to being hung over.

7. Alicia suspects that something has been added to her coffee when Alexander picks up her cup by mistake and his mother immediately reacts to his drinking from the wrong cup.

8. Alexander is the one who decides that Alicia is to be killed.

QUIZ **41**

The Paradine Case

SELZNICK/VANGUARD/UNITED ARTISTS (1947), B&W, 85 MINUTES

The Paradine Case was the last film Hitchcock directed for Hollywood's famed producer David O. Selznick. The tension between them had grown insurmountable over their several years together, as the two were unable to agree creatively on much of anything. After almost a year of arguing over the plot characterization, Selznick decided to rewrite the entire script just as production started. The cast received the new dialogue each morning and had to be ready on the spur of the moment. This unorganized method of filming almost drove Hitchcock mad, until he took a lackadaisical attitude toward the film, often appearing to be dozing in his director's chair while on the set. The following quiz contains five short-answer questions.

1. Why is Maddalena Paradine arrested?

2. What is Mr. Paradine's handicap?

3. How is the poison administered to Mr. Paradine?

4. What strategy does Anthony Keane use to prove that his client is innocent of murdering her husband?

5. What tragic incident causes Maddalena to confess to the crime?

QUIZ **42**

Rope

TRANSATLANTIC/WARNER BROS. (1948), COLOR, 81 MINUTES

Hitchcock always had a profound curiosity about avant-garde and alternative lifestyles. Although the homosexual relationship between the two leading men in *Rope* is revealed only in subtle nuances to circumvent the Hollywood film production code, just the idea of filming (or even suggesting) alternative lifestyles was a very bold undertaking for any producer or director in late 1940s Hollywood. The following quiz contains ten true/false statements.

1. David's body is hidden in the living room chest.

2. Rupert Cadell used to be a private tutor to both Philip and Brandon.

3. Rupert is now a magazine editor.

4. Philip is a painter.

5. When Mrs. Atwell is reading Philip's palm, she predicts that his hands will bring him disaster.

6. Janet, David's fiancée, works for *Life* magazine.

7. The group discusses the philosophy of Immanuel Kant.

8. Brandon's excuse for moving the dinner party into the living room is so that they can view the city's skyline.

9. Rupert's suspicions are confirmed when he notices David's coat in the closet.

10. Rupert leaves his cigarette case in the apartment, giving himself an excuse for returning.

QUIZ **43**

Under Capricorn

TRANSATLANTIC/WARNER BROS. (1949), COLOR, 117 MINUTES

Under Capricorn was the second and last film made by Hitchcock's and producer Sidney Bernstein's company, Transatlantic Pictures. In making this movie, Hitchcock was looking for the perfect screen vehicle for favored movie star Ingrid Bergman. However, the relationship between Hitchcock and Bergman grew tense during the shoot. The married Bergman was struggling with the ramifications of her scandalous romantic involvement with Italian film director Roberto Rossellini, and Hitchcock was brooding over his unrequited love for his beautiful, bright leading lady.

During the filming of the scene where Bergman is to make a drunken descent down the staircase, actress and director argued over whether it was necessary for her to stay exactly on the stair marks he had so precisely designated. Hitchcock agreed to shoot both his version and hers, and upon reviewing the rushes, she could decide which was better. Bergman conceded to Hitchcock's take, but the atmosphere of discontent was pervasive throughout the shoot. The following quiz contains ten multiple choice questions.

1. Why does Sam give Charles £1,000 to buy a piece of land?
   A. Charles reminds Sam of himself when he first came to Sydney.
   B. Sam is trying to get on the good side of the governor through his nephew, Charles.
   C. Sam wants to buy the land for himself, but he has already purchased his allotted amount.
   D. Sam cannot purchase land because he has been in prison.

2. Why is Sam ostracized by the community?
   A. His business dealings ruined many local businessmen.
   B. He served time in prison.
   C. Lady Henrietta has a drinking problem and often causes a scene.
   D. He is illegitimate.

3. Why does Lady Henrietta Flusky's presence at the dinner party cause a stir?
   A. She wears a gown that is too revealing for polite society.
   B. She has not been seen in public for several years.
   C. She is drunk and barefooted.
   D. She comes to the table in a state of rage and fights with her husband.

4. How do Henrietta Flusky and Charles know one another?
   A. They are cousins.
   B. They were friends when they lived in Ireland.
   C. They were in love when they were young.
   D. They grew up on neighboring estates.

5. What does Lady Henrietta do to show that she is in charge of the household staff?
   A. She fires the cook.
   B. She goes into the kitchen and attempts to give the orders for the day.
   C. She demands that Milly show her all the household accounts.
   D. She dresses, goes to her office, and starts organizing her much-neglected correspondence.

6. Why does Milly leave the service of Lady Henrietta?
   A. Lady Henrietta fires her.
   B. She leaves out of frustration because of Lady Henrietta's newfound power.
   C. She tells Sam that she loves him, and as a result, he asks her to leave.
   D. Charles knows what she is doing and threatens to expose her if she does not leave.

7. How do Sam and Lady Henrietta manage to get an invitation to the governor's ball without the governor's knowledge?
   A. Charles forges their names on an invitation.
   B. The governor's wife sends the invitation.
   C. Sam and Lady Henrietta go as Charles' guest.
   D. Charles adds their names to the guest list after it has been approved by the governor.

8. How did Lady Henrietta's brother really die?
   A. Lady Henrietta's father killed him.
   B. He committed suicide.
   C. Lady Henrietta killed him.
   D. Charles killed him.

9. Why does Sam shoot Charles?
   A. He is afraid Charles is going to turn him over to the police.
   B. He misunderstands the embrace between Charles and Henrietta.
   C. He fears Charles and Henrietta are planning to leave together.
   D. He shoots Charles by accident when Charles tries to take the gun away from him.

10. How does Lady Henrietta come to realize that Milly is her enemy?
    A. She sees Milly put the shrunken head in its box and then pour all of the sleeping medication into Lady Henrietta's drink.
    B. She overhears Milly planning to sabotage her marriage.
    C. She realizes that Milly has adjusted the household accounts to make it seem that she has been overspending her budget.
    D. Charles tells her that he saw Milly trying on her clothes and laughing.

CHAPTER 5

The 1950s—
Becoming a Legend

*"People don't always express their inner
thoughts to one another; a conversation may
be quite trivial, but often the eyes will
reveal what a person really thinks or feels."*

ALFRED HITCHCOCK, 1967

AS ALFRED HITCHCOCK NOW BRANCHED INTO DIFFERENT
media and personal investments, the 1950s proved to be the most
prolific and financially successful decade thus far for the film director. He
released eleven feature films, directed several teleplays, and helped establish the awarding-winning CBS-TV series, *Alfred Hitchcock Presents*. He
also lent his name to a new publication, *Alfred Hitchcock's Mystery
Magazine*. The beginning of the fifties also found him involved in a cattle
ranch, a vineyard in northern California, and investments in stocks and
oil. Although increasing his wealth, these activities did nothing for his
depression over not being in the director's chair. Though having signed a
multipicture deal with Jack Warner, there still was no promise of a project
in the immediate future.

Hitchcock's film career also suffered from the box-office failures of *Under Capricorn* (1949) and *Stage Fright* (1950). However, his creative mind was rekindled upon his discovery of Patricia Highsmith's novel, *Strangers on a Train*. He adapted it for the screen, released it in 1951, and received both public and critical acclaim for his efforts. It reestablished him as the creator of superb, spine-tingling thrillers. Except for *I Confess* (1953) and *The Wrong Man* (1957), which were each moderately successful, every Hitchcock film released in the fifties became a box-office hit. He also established personal and professional relationships with actors whose names have become inextricably linked with his—Grace Kelly, James Stewart, and Cary Grant.

Though the early 1950s found the American film industry in a downturn due to the rising appeal of the completely new medium, television, Hollywood nonetheless put its faith in Hitchcock. He signed another multi-picture deal, this time with Paramount for five feature films. With the release of *Rear Window* (1954) and *To Catch a Thief* (1955), Hitchcock lured television audiences back to the theatres. Both releases were extremely successful, and Hitchcock was finally given the power, freedom, and money he sought to create his screen masterpieces.

In the summer of 1959 he undertook a project which emerged as his most popular screen work ever, the thriller/horror masterpiece *Psycho*. Film buffs believe that this picture reveals Hitchcock's innermost thoughts and intimate feelings. Released in 1960, it guaranteed the moviemaker's prosperity for the rest of his life.

QUIZ **44**

Stage Fright

WARNER BROS. (1950), B&W, 110 MINUTES

During the filming of *Stage Fright*, Hitchcock had difficulty preventing costar Jane Wyman from glamorizing herself too much. She played the role of plain, wholesome Eve Gill, but did not like being overshadowed by Marlene Dietrich, cast as the gorgeous femme fatale of this thriller. The following quiz contains ten true/false statements.

1. Charlotte lures Johnny to the murder scene by pleading with him to return and retrieve her earring.

2. A neighbor sees Johnny running from the house where the murder was committed.

3. To link Charlotte to the crime, Johnny does not immediately destroy her bloodstained dress.

4. Eve's father notices that the bloodstain was deliberately placed on the dress.

5. Eve is portraying Lady Macbeth, her first role as an actress.

6. In order to get close to Charlotte and gain vital information to prove Johnny's innocence, Eve takes a job as understudy to Charlotte.

7. Eve's mother compares Inspector Smith's piano playing to Sherlock Holmes' playing the violin in order to help him concentrate on solving a crime.

8. Inspector Smith wants Eve to call him Sherlock Holmes.

9. Eve's father manages to hide Inspector Smith in a trunk in Charlotte's dressing room so that he can overhear Charlotte's confession to the murder.

10. Charlotte convinces Johnny to kill her husband by bribing him with half of the insurance money.

QUIZ 45

Strangers on a Train

WARNER BROS. (1951), B&W, 103 MINUTES

Alfred Hitchcock's creative genius and experience allowed him to film the entire movie in his mind before production started. By this point, for him, the best part of making the movie was over. As a result, he often appeared moody and withdrawn on his sets. For example, the second day of filming *Stranger on a Train*, actor Farley Granger asked Hitchcock why he was moping. Hitchcock's response was, "I'm so bored. I've done it all, Farley, you know that." The following quiz contains multiple choice questions.

1. Of what exciting occurrence in Bruno's life is he most proud?
   A. He has played Russian roulette three times and survived.
   B. He broke into his grandmother's house while she was asleep and rummaged through her closet looking for her will.
   C. He drove a car 150 miles per hour while blindfolded.
   D. He dove fifty feet from a bridge into a river.

2. What fantastic voyage does Bruno plan to take in the future?
   A. He plans to make reservations on the first rocket ship to the moon.
   B. He plans to travel around the world by rail.
   C. He plans to travel across the Sahara on foot.
   D. He plans to travel through Europe spending none of his own money.

3. What kindly, but ironic gesture does Bruno perform immediately after committing murder?
   A. He straightens Miriam's clothes and fixes her hair.
   B. He helps Miriam's neighbor carry in her groceries.
   C. He helps a blind man cross the street.
   D. He drops some coins in a panhandler's cup.

4. At what time is the murder committed?
   A. Midnight
   C. 9:20–9:25 P.M.
   B. 4:44 A.M.
   D. 11:15 P.M.

5. What does Bruno deliver to Guy proving that Bruno has killed Miriam?
   A. Miriam's glasses
   B. The bracelet Guy had given Miriam
   C. Miriam's alarm clock with the time of the murder frozen on the dial
   D. The scarf Miriam was wearing when she was killed

6. What is significant about Bruno's tie clip?
   A. It is identical to the one Guy always wears.
   B. It is scratched and bent.
   C. It has his name engraved on it.
   D. It belonged to his father.

7. Of whom does Barbara remind Bruno?
   A. His mother
   C. His last victim
   B. His wife
   D. Miriam

8. What three things does Bruno send Guy through the mail?
   A. A glass ornament, a wine glass, and a paperweight, all containing Guy's fingerprints
   B. A picture of Guy and his new lover, a copy of his wife's insurance policy, and a letter Guy wrote to Miriam demanding a divorce
   C. Travel brochures, his passport, and the card of a travel agent
   D. A key to Bruno's house, a map of the inside of the house, and, in a second delivery, a gun

9. Why does Guy sneak into the Anthony home?
   A. He wants to tell Bruno's father what Bruno has done.
   B. He wants to return the items he received from Bruno.
   C. He is looking for evidence to prove his innocence.
   D. He hopes to uncover Bruno's true identity.

10. How does Barbara create a diversion, stalling the police so Guy can leave the tennis courts unnoticed?

   A. She parks her car behind the police car, blocking its exit.

   B. She claims her purse has just been stolen and demands their immediate assistance.

   C. She bumps into the policeman, spilling the powder from her compact all over his pants.

   D. She pretends to faint.

11. On which ride in the carnival do Bruno and Guy fight?

   A. The Ferris wheel

   B. A boat going through the tunnel of love

   C. The roller coaster

   D. The carousel

12. Who recognizes Bruno as the one at the scene of the crime the night the murder was committed?

   A. A man who works at the carnival

   B. Miriam's friend

   C. A little boy who was at the carnival on the night of the murder

   D. A security guard

QUIZ 46

I Confess

WARNER BROS. (1953), B&W, 95 MINUTES

To play the key part of Ruth Grandfort in *I Confess*, Hitchcock wanted to cast a foreign actress with a European accent, so he hired Swedish actress Anita Bjork two weeks before shooting began. When she arrived in the United States with a lover and an illegitimate baby in tow, Warner Bros. was appalled and fired her. At the last minute, Hitchcock hired Anne Baxter to replace Bjork. The following quiz contains ten short-answer questions.

1. Why does Otto Keller kill Mr. Villette?

2. Why are the police skeptical that robbery was the motive for the murder?

3. What leads the police to suspect Father Logan of the murder?

4. What ended the affair between Ruth and Father Logan?

5. Why does Ruth's confession not prevent Father Logan from being arrested for Villette's murder?

6. Why is Villette blackmailing Ruth Grandfort?

7. What does Villette threaten to tell Ruth's husband?

8. What does Keller do to ensure that Father Logan is convicted of Villette's murder?

9. How does Inspector Larrue find out the truth about what really happened on the night of Villette's murder?

10. What are Mrs. Keller and Otto Keller's last words before they die?

QUIZ **47**

Dial M for Murder

WARNER BROS. (1954), COLOR, 105 MINUTES

In 1953, Hitchcock was working on the script for a film based on a story by David Duncan called "The Bramble Bush." The tale concerned a man who takes the identity of another, only to discover that the other person is wanted for murder. However, Hitchcock had trouble making the script work and abandoned the idea. Needing a film to quickly replace "The Bramble Bush," Hitchcock undertook the hit London-Broadway play *Dial M for Murder*. Although unenthusiastic about making this movie, shot in the then-innovative 3-D process, he was rewarded by securing Grace Kelly to play the female lead. She also starred in his next two feature films and became a close friend of the Hitchcocks, remaining so even after her marriage to Monaco's Prince Rainier. The following quiz contains twelve true/false questions.

1. Tony wants to have Margot murdered so that he can inherit her money.

2. Tony persuades Swan to come to his apartment by pretending he wants to buy insurance from Swan.

3. Tony offers to pay Swan £1,000 to murder his wife.

4. Tony leaves a key in the hall, under the carpet on the stair.

5. The murder is to take place at five minutes after midnight.

6. Tony calls Margot to get her to the desk and in the right position for Swan to reach from behind the curtain and strangle her.

7. Swan is to whistle into the phone to signal Tony that he has completed his mission.

8. Tony plans Margot's murder to look like a suicide.

9. Margot stabs Swan with a letter opener.

10. Inspector Hubbard asks Mark for an autograph in order to match his handwriting with that of a love letter to Margot.

11. The jury sentences Margot to life in prison.

12. Inspector Hubbard knows Margot is innocent when she uses the key in her purse to try to open the door.

QUIZ 48

Rear Window

PARAMOUNT (1954), COLOR, 113 MINUTES

Only a few weeks before the scheduled shooting of *Rear Window*, Grace Kelly received a call from her talent agent informing her that Hitchcock had arranged for her wardrobe fitting for the female lead opposite Jimmy Stewart. Kelly, about to sign a contract for a lead role in Elia Kazan's *On the Waterfront* (1954) at Columbia Pictures, was forced to make a decision quickly. She read Hitchcock's script that afternoon, turned down Elia Kazan's offer (which went to Eva Marie Saint who won an Oscar for her work), and flew to Los Angeles to begin working on her second Hitchcock movie. The following quiz contains fifteen multiple choice questions.

1. How did Jeffries break his left leg?
   A. Falling off an elephant while stalking tigers in India
   B. Taking pictures at an auto race when a race car spun out of control and careened into the press stand
   C. Trekking in the Himalayas
   D. Skiing in the Catskills

2. What is written on his cast?
   A. A get-well verse from Lisa
   B. The scheduled date for the removal of the cast
   C. "Here lie the broken bones of L. B. Jeffries."
   D. "A man's home is his castle."

3. From which New York restaurant does Lisa order their dinner?
   A. 21   B. The Russian Tea Room
   C. Sardi's   D. The Waldorf

4. How many times does Thorwald leave his apartment carrying his sample case?

 A. Three—two times in the middle of the night and once the next morning

 B. He leaves his apartment many times that night, but only once is he carrying his sample case.

 C. He moves his sample case from one room to another, but the audience never actually sees him take it from the apartment.

 D. He draws attention to himself by lugging the case from his apartment four times during the middle of the night.

5. As a traveling salesman, what items does Thorwald sell?

 A. Watches   B. Brushes

 C. Perfume   D. Costume jewelry

6. What is in the trunk that Thorwald removes from his apartment the next day?

 A. Mrs. Thorwald's clothes

 B. Mrs. Thorwald's collection of murder mysteries

 C. Cutting tools

 D. Nothing; the trunk is empty.

7. Why does Jeffries suspect that Thorwald is the man who killed his neighbor's dog?

 A. Thorwald closes his blinds when the owner discovers her dead canine.

 B. Thorwald has always hated the dog, and kicked it on at least one occasion.

 C. When the owner finds her pet dead in the garden, all the neighbors, except Thorwald, respond to her screams.

 D. At the moment the owner discovers her dog dead, Jeffries happens to be watching Thorwald through his binoculars and notices that Thorwald is smirking.

8. Why is Lisa suspicious of Thorwald?
   A. She realizes Thorwald's wife did not take her favorite handbag or jewelry with her when she left.
   B. She sees Thorwald leaving his apartment with another woman.
   C. Thorwald turns facedown a picture of his wife that is sitting on the dresser.
   D. Thorwald is no longer wearing his wedding ring.

9. What is in the note that Jeffries writes to Thorwald?
   A. "I saw what you did."
   B. "What have you done with her?"
   C. "I've been watching you."
   D. "I know where your wife *really* is."

10. How is Jeffries planning to signal Lisa and Stella that Thorwald is on his way back into his apartment?
    A. He will call Thorwald's apartment.
    B. He will turn on the light in his apartment.
    C. He will open and close his blinds.
    D. He will set off a flashbulb on his camera.

11. What is the crisis that is about to occur in a neighbor's apartment that is ignored by Jeffries and Lisa because their attention is on Thorwald?
    A. A violent domestic dispute occurs between the newlyweds.
    B. The dancer is being attacked by a man she brought home.
    C. Miss Lonelyhearts is about to take an overdose of pills.
    D. The musician is about to set fire to a stack of his original music.

12. What does Thorwald say when he enters Jeffries' apartment?
    A. "You're next."   B. "Who are you?"
    C. "The joke's on you."   D. "What do you want from me?"

13. How does Jeffries try to defend himself when Thorwald comes after him?
    A. He grabs a pair of scissors.
    B. He tries to strike Thorwald with his crutches.
    C. He starts throwing his camera lenses at Thorwald.
    D. He sets off flashbulbs in Thorwald's eyes trying to blind him.

14. What is in the hatbox?
    A. Mrs. Thorwald's purse and wedding ring
    B. A bloody dagger
    C. The contents are never disclosed. ∕
    D. Mrs. Thorwald's head

15. What is Lisa doing at the end of the film in order to show an apparent interest in Jeffries' lifestyle?
    A. She is perusing a brochure on photography lessons.
    B. She is trying on a new pair of hiking boots.
    C. She is reading a book entitled *Beyond the High Himalayas*.
    D. She is reading a *National Geographic* magazine. ∕

QUIZ **49**

To Catch a Thief

PARAMOUNT (1955), COLOR, 103 MINUTES

The sophisticated *To Catch a Thief* was shot in the new widescreen Vista-Vision process. The oncamera conversation between costars Cary Grant and Grace Kelly during the famous picnic scene in the car overlooking the Riviera was impromptu and unrehearsed. Hitchcock shot three takes of the sequence, each with different spontaneous dialogue (full of double entendres). The only difficulty was in deciding which to use, because the director was delighted by all three. The following quiz contains eight true/false statements.

1. John Robie not only used to be a jewel thief, but was also a member of the Resistance during World War II.

2. John's skill as a cat burglar came from his childhood when he used to go mountain climbing with his father.

3. Lloyd's of London contacts John Robie to convince him to pretend to return to his former profession in order to find the real cat burglar.

4. When John meets Mrs. Stevens and her daughter, Frances, he tells them he owns a coffee plantation in Africa.

5. Mrs. Stevens and Frances are wealthy because oil was discovered on their property just after Mr. Stevens died.

6. John receives the following message from the copycat burglar: "Robie, you've already used up eight of your nine lives. Don't gamble your last one."

7. John knows where the next burglary is to take place because he receives an anonymous tip delivered in a croissant.

8. It is not possible that Foussard, the wine steward, is the cat burglar because he has a wooden leg and cannot scale the steep rooftops.

QUIZ 50

The Trouble with Harry

PARAMOUNT (1955), COLOR, 100 MINUTES

The Trouble with Harry is an American comedy with an English flair. The humor is dry, with very nonchalant attitudes toward serious subjects such as death and sex. The wry film, starring John Forsythe and movie newcomer Shirley MacLaine, did not go over well with audiences in the United States, but was a success in England. The following quiz contains twelve short-answer questions.

1. How many shots are fired in the woods on the day Harry dies?

2. Who steals Harry's shoes?

3. What peculiar smoking habit does Sam have?

4. How does Sam discover the corpse?

5. What question does Arnie ask Sam about the birds and the bees?

6. Why did Jennifer leave her second husband?

7. Why does the Captain want to dig up Harry immediately after he and Sam buried him?

8. Who confesses to killing Harry?

9. Why do Sam, Jennifer, Miss Graveley, and the Captain decide to bury Harry again?

10. Where do they hide Harry's body when Calvin Wiggs comes to investigate?

11. For what does Sam eventually trade his paintings?

12. How did Harry die?

QUIZ 51

The Man Who Knew Too Much

PARAMOUNT (1956), COLOR, 120 MINUTES

Twenty-two years after the British-filmed original, Hitchcock remade *The Man Who Knew Too Much*, this time in color, stereophonic sound, and in the VistaVision widescreen process.

During this retooling of *The Man Who Knew Too Much*, Hitchcock, after almost fifteen years in the United States, decided to become an American citizen. Anxious not to lose any time filming, Hitchcock asked his art director, Henry Bumstead, if it were possible for the judge to come to the studio to personally administer the oath of citizenship to Hitchcock. The filmmaker also argued that he should not have to appear in court with "common" immigrants. His colleagues convinced him that this request was inappropriate. Hitchcock acquiesced and appeared at the Los Angeles County Courthouse for his swearing in on April 20, 1955. The following quiz contains twelve multiple choice questions.

1. In what part of Africa does the movie open?
   A. Cairo, Egypt   B. Algiers, Algeria
   C. Timbuktu, Mali   D. Marrakech, Morocco

2. Where do Ben and Jo McKenna meet Louis Bernard?
   A. On a bus
   B. In the market
   C. In the hotel when they ask him for directions
   D. At the airport

3. What career did Jo give up for her family?
   A. Film star   B. Singer
   C. Stage actress   D. Dancer

4. How is Louis Bernard disguised when he is murdered?
   A. As a Muslim woman   B. As a street beggar
   C. As a street juggler   D. As an Arab

5. When does Ben first realize Hank has been kidnapped?
   A. He is given a note from the kidnappers.
   B. He receives a call from the kidnappers while he is at the police station.
   C. After he and Jo return to the hotel, Ben receives a call from Hank telling him that he has been kidnapped.
   D. Mrs. Drayton leaves a note in the hotel room telling him that Hank will be "taken care of" if Ben does not cooperate.

6. How does Ben prepare Jo for the news that Hank has been kidnapped?
   A. He tells Jo to drink a glass of brandy.
   B. He suggests that Jo sit down and take a deep breath. ✓
   C. He gives Jo a sedative.
   D. He sits beside Jo and holds her hands.

7. How does Jo come to realize that Ambrose Chappell is a place instead of a person?
   A. She picks up the Bible and realizes that Ambrose Chapel may be a church.

   B. A friend mentions that Ben is searching for a man named Church. Upon hearing the word "church," she realizes that Ambrose Chapel is a chapel, not a person.
   C. She is staring out the window at a church tower, when the idea comes to her.
   D. Her friends are making puns and she realizes that a word could have more than one meaning. ✓

8. What leads Jo to Albert Hall?
   A. She reads in the newspaper that the prime minister is attending a concert at Albert Hall.
   B. She remembers Ben mentioning Albert Hall in a previous conversation. ✓
   C. She calls the police station to ask for help and is told that he is attending a concert at Albert Hall.
   D. She suspects that the kidnappers may be there.

9. How does Ben escape from Ambrose Chapel?

   A. He climbs the rope attached to the church bell.
   B. He smashes the lock with an iron pipe.
   C. He breaks a window and crawls down vines that are growing on the wall. ✓
   D. He crawls through a ventilation duct onto the roof.

10. How does Jo foil the assassination attempt?
    A. She sends a message to the prime minister via the theatre manager.
    B. She pushes the prime minister down just as the assassin pulls the trigger.
    C. She screams and distracts the audience, causing the assassin to miss his chance to fire the fatal shot.
    D. She manages to get behind the assassin and shove him, causing the bullet to go astray.

11. What is the song Jo sings that alerts Hank that she is at the embassy?
    A. *Star Spangled Banner*   B. *God Bless America*
    C. *We'll Love Again*   D. *Que Será, Será*

12. What does Mrs. Drayton tell Hank to do to signal his parents that he is near?
    A. Tap on the walls
    B. Whistle the same song that his mother is singing
    C. Play his favorite tune on the piano
    D. Wave his cap out of the window

QUIZ 52

The Wrong Man
WARNER BROS. (1957), B&W, 105 MINUTES

"Vera is the girl who is going to replace Grace Kelly," proclaimed Hitchcock as he introduced his new leading lady to the press. Feeling rejected over Kelly's decision to abandon her Hollywood career and marry Prince Rainier of Monaco, Hitchcock turned his attentions to rising actress Vera Miles. However, Miles did not have the confidence, as Kelly did, to put Hitchcock in his place when he demanded from her long hours for his "personal" coaching. As a result, the relationship between Hitchcock and his new star was constantly strained and tense. The following quiz contains eight true/false questions.

1. Manny is the trombone player in the band.

2. Manny is trying to borrow money on Rose's insurance policy to pay for her operation.

3. Manny is arrested because an office clerk at the insurance company thought she recognized him as the man who held her up.

4. Manny misspells "drawer," which causes the police to believe that Manny is responsible for the robberies.

5. The police ask the robbery victims to identify Manny by showing them his picture.

6. Manny and Rose go to the club where Manny works, hoping to find a witness to establish Manny's innocence.

7. Manny is unable to establish an alibi because two of the possible witnesses have died.

8. Rose has a nervous breakdown because she believes Manny is guilty.

QUIZ 53

Vertigo

PARAMOUNT (1958), COLOR, 128 MINUTES

Hitchcock, the great director, was not above performing childish pranks when forced to comply with the studio's demands. When Paramount cast Kim Novak in the role of Madeleine/Judy in *Vertigo*, Hitchcock retaliated by taunting the inexperienced actress. He refused to direct her in the complex dual role, and horrified her by hanging a dead chicken over her dressing room mirror. Today, Novak has forgiven the "master" and regards Hitchcock's refusal to direct her as a liberating professional experience. "It allowed the freedom to bring me into it," says the now retired actress, currently living in Oregon with her veterinarian husband. "Hitchcock gave me technique; I gave him my raw feelings. The combination is what makes the movie work." The following quiz contains twelve short-answer questions.

1. Why does Gavin Elster want his wife, Madeleine, followed?

2. What does Elster fear is wrong with his wife?

3. Whose grave does Madeleine visit on the day that Scottie follows her?

4. What is the title of the portrait Madeleine visits in the museum?

5. To which bookstore does Midge take Scottie to find out about the name on the tombstone?

6. Where does Madeleine's dream take her and Scottie?

7. What is the verdict at the inquest concerning Madeleine's death?

8. What happens to Scottie after he believes that Madeleine has died?

9. Where does Scottie find Judy Barton?

10. What does Scottie want to change about Judy's appearance and why?

11. When does Scottie realize that Madeleine and Judy are the same person?

12. What causes Judy to fall from the church tower?

Trivia Facts:
Did You Know That . . .

Just Relax and Enjoy the View—During the filming of *Strangers on a Train* (1951), Hitchcock's daughter, Patricia, was stranded at the top of the Ferris wheel at night, according to her father's instructions. He had planned this event as a practical joke, but Patricia was brought down when she became hysterical.

Cinderella Meets Prince Charming—Grace Kelly met Prince Rainier of Monaco, her future husband, while on the French Riviera filming *To Catch a Thief* (1955).

Acting for Two or Acting as Two?—Blonde Vera Miles, a Hitchcock favorite, was to play Judy/Madeleine in *Vertigo* (1958), but was forced to cancel her assignment when it was discovered that she was pregnant. She was replaced by Kim Novak.

Don't Let the Size Fool You—Even though *Rear Window* was shot in L. B. Jeffries' (Jimmy Stewart's) one-room apartment, the set for the entire film was one of the largest ever built at Paramount. Each of the thirty-one apartments across the courtyard into which Jeffries gazes, twelve of which were completely furnished, had to be constructed according to Hitchcock's specifications.

Don't Try This at Home—During the lensing of the rooftop scene in *To Catch a Thief*, Hitchcock requested that screenwriter John Michael Hayes accompany him to the top of the scaffolding. Thinking that they were to discuss a particular shot, Hayes was surprised to learn that Hitchcock wanted only to find out if Hayes was as frightened of heights as he was.

It Was Not Yet His Time—While filming in a gymnasium on a temporary sound stage, due to inclement weather, Hitchcock almost met an early demise making *The Trouble with Harry* (1955), when an 850-pound camera fell from a crane, grazing the director's shoulder.

Don't Create a Problem Where There Isn't One—Doris Day almost quit during the filming of *The Man Who Knew Too Much* (1956), a remake of the earlier 1934 Hitchcock movie. The star was upset because Hitchcock had not given her any feedback on the quality of her performance. Assuming that he was dissatisfied with her acting, Day approached him ready to resign her key role. Astonished, he told her that her work was perfect, and that if she were not performing to his satisfaction he would certainly have told her so.

Improved with Age—*Rear Window*, re-released in 1983, brought in $9.1 million at the box office.

Woman of Many Talents—Hitchcock's wife, Alma, plotted the intricate car chase between John Robie (Cary Grant) and the police in the movie *To Catch a Thief*.

Under Control—Hitchcock hired Hollywood designer Edith Head to design offcamera clothes for his favorite leading ladies, thus dictating what they should wear both on and off the set.

The Best Part of the Day—During the filming of *Foreign Correspondent* (1940), Hitchcock developed the routine of eating a seven-course meal along with wine for lunch, which sometimes caused him to fall asleep during the filming.

The American Dream—Hitchcock loved American food and would often eat, in one sitting, several hot dogs covered with sauerkraut.

QUIZ **54**

North by Northwest

MGM (1959), COLOR, 137 MINUTES

Favorite Hitchcock themes (the paranoia that accompanies losing one's identity, being falsely accused of a crime, and not knowing whom to trust) are all showcased in one critically acclaimed film—*North by Northwest*. The efforts of Alfred Hitchcock and Cary Grant in making this thriller were considered phenomenal. Was Grant's flawless performance attributed to his insight into Hitchcock's vision? Or, was his success in playing the lost hero due to a deep understanding of the plot? Toward the end of the film, Grant said to Hitchcock, "Look here, Hitch, I've read this script dozens of times, and I'm damned if I can figure it out." Maybe the success of *North by Northwest*, shot in the VistaVision widescreen process, was for simpler reasons than we realized! The following quiz contains sixteen multiple choice questions.

1. What is Roger Thornhill's occupation?
   A. Accountant   B. Advertising executive
   C. Exporter   D. Banker

2. Why is Roger mistaken for George Kaplan?
   A. There is a mix-up in the restaurant and he is seated at a table reserved for George Kaplan.
   B. He is wearing the exact tie that Kaplan is supposed to have worn.
   C. He raises his hand for the waiter to bring him a phone at the same time George Kaplan is being paged.
   D. He uses an unusual word that happens to be the password for identifying George Kaplan.

3. How do Roger's enemies try to get rid of him?

    A. They force him to swallow large amounts of bourbon and then try to push his car over a cliff.

    B. They tamper with the brakes on his car and try to force him off the road and over a cliff.

    C. They plan to get him drunk and run over him, making his death appear as a hit-and-run.

    D. They plan to shoot him, making it look as if he were a burglar.

4. What hapzpens when Roger, his mother, and the detectives go back to the mansion to check out Roger's kidnapping story?

    A. The mansion is boarded up.

    B. A different family is living there, and they say that they have never seen Roger before.

    C. A woman claiming to be Mrs. Townsend says that Roger attended her party the previous night and that he was too drunk to drive home.

    D. The butler answers the door and says that the family is traveling in Europe.

5. Where does Roger locate the real Lester Townsend?

    A. At the United Nations

    B. At the restaurant where Roger was mistaken for Kaplan

    C. In an office in the Empire State Building

    D. At Grand Central Station

6. Why do the police believe Roger killed Lester Townsend?

    A. A witness claims he saw Roger stab Townsend.

    B. After he is stabbed, Townsend falls into Roger's arms, and Roger unconsciously pulls out the knife.

    C. Roger is carrying Townsend's picture.

    D. Roger is running away from the scene of the crime.

7. Where and how do Eve Kendall and Roger meet?
   A. They meet at the train station when Roger bumps into Eve causing her to spill the contents of her suitcase.
   B. They meet in the train's dining car when Roger invites himself to join her for dinner.
   C. They meet on the train when Roger ducks into her compartment, trying to avoid the police.
   D. They meet at the ticket office when Roger cuts in front of Eve.

8. What excuse does Roger give Eve for running from the police?
   A. He is a serial killer.   B. He has overdue parking tickets.
   C. He is wanted for bigamy.   D. He robbed a candy store.

9. How do Roger and Eve end up sitting at the same table in the dining car?
   A. Eve bribes the maitre d' to seat Roger at her table.
   B. Roger waits until the dining car is full before he sits down with Eve, claiming that there are no available tables.
   C. Eve makes a place card with his name and a noose drawn on it.
   D. Roger tells the waiter that Eve is his wife.

10. Roger's matches and handkerchief are monogrammed with the letters ROT. What does he tell Eve the O stands for?
   A. Zero   B. Obey
   C. Nothing   D. Obstinate

11. How does Roger manage to escape from the plane that is trying to run him down?
   A. He takes shelter in a barn.
   B. He stops a gasoline truck, causing the plane to fly into it and explode.
   C. He runs toward a power line, causing the plane to fly into it and crash.
   D. He runs through a pasture, flushing out a covey of quail, causing them to fly into the engine of the plane.

12. How does Roger know where Eve is going when she sneaks out of her hotel room?
    A. Using a pencil, he shades over the address Eve wrote on the telephone pad.
    B. He overhears her telephone conversation while he is hidden in the bathroom.
    C. He looks through her address book and finds an address written on that day's date.
    D. He reads a letter that is in her purse.

13. Who is the real George Kaplan?
    A. The professor   B. Vandamm
    C. Eve   D. He doesn't exist.

14. How does Eve realize that Vandamm is wise to her deception?
    A. Roger slips a note in her handbag, warning her of Vandamm's intentions.
    B. Roger writes a note on the inside of his matchbook and throws it over the balcony to where she is sitting in the living room.
    C. Roger sneaks up to her window and mimes a warning.
    D. Eve sees Roger motioning to her from the top of the stairs.

15. How does the housekeeper know that Roger is in the house?
    A. She finds him sneaking in through an upstairs window.
    B. She spots him in the hall mirror.
    C. She interrupts his message to Eve.
    D. She sees his reflection in the television screen.

16. How does Roger encourage Eve to hang on so that he can pull her to safety when she is hanging from a ledge on Mount Rushmore?
    A. He proposes to her by calling her Mrs. Thornhill.
    B. He begs her to hang on because he loves her.
    C. He tells her to hang on so she can spend the rest of her life thanking him.
    D. He advises her to hang on or he will jump off after her.

CHAPTER **6**

The 1960s—
The Turning point

"I like everything around me to be clear as crystal and

completely calm. I don't want clouds overhead. I get

a feeling of inner peace from a well-organized

desk . . . . I've always dreamed of the day I wouldn't

have to see the rushes at all!"

ALFRED HITCHCOCK, 1967

*P*SYCHO (1960) DISPLAYS A CLEAR, DEFINITIVE
craftsmanship that reflects the director's ability to conceptualize technical scenes. The shower scene in the black-and-white *Psycho* is probably the most memorable sequence of any Hitchcock film. Most of us vividly recall the shock-effect that lingered long after we left the theatre, and we swore we would never take another shower as long as we lived. With its shrieking sounds forever resounding in our memory, and the irony of Norman Bates' boyish innocence as he watches Marion's car slowly sink into the water horrifying us, the film was the perfect thriller—full of symbolism, shock, and of course, surprise.

The sixties saw the release of only five new Hitchcock feature films. After *Psycho*, Hitchcock struggled to get his next two screen projects off the ground. While searching for the perfect actress to portray the leading role in *Marnie* (1964), Hitchcock came across two bizarre newspaper articles that appealed to his fascination with birds. Each article described strange occurrences in which flocks of birds attacked people. Were these incidents an omen? Several years earlier, Hitchcock had purchased the film rights to Daphne du Maurier's short story, *The Birds*. Hitchcock was so enthusiastic that he put *Marnie* on the back burner and set out to make a film that would "scare the hell out of people"—even more than *Psycho*.

Tippi Hedren, Hitchcock's leading lady for *The Birds* (1963), had never acted in films before. He wanted to mold the former model into his next brilliant star. However, his fascination with the blonde Ms. Hedren turned into a dark obsession that nearly ruined her career and left him emotionally drained. It was a devastating personal experience from which he never fully recovered. Tippi Hedren also subsequently starred in *Marnie*, but after Hitchcock's obsession with his actress intensified, she severed her professional relationship with him forever.

Hitchcock made two more movies during the 1960s, *Torn Curtain* (1966) and *Topaz* (1969), both of which were critical and commercial disappointments. Clouds were beginning to form over Hitchcock's career and his clarity and vision were beginning to fade. Now, more than ever, he needed the assistance of others, both personally and professionally.

QUIZ **55**

Psycho

PARAMOUNT (1960), B&W, 168 MINUTES

In searching for the perfect sound effects for the legendary shower scene, Hitchcock sent a prop man for a watermelon. Understanding Hitchcock's intention, the prop man returned not only with one watermelon, but with a variety of melons. After listening, with his eyes closed, to the stabbing of one fruit after another, Hitchcock made his selection known by uttering one word, "Casaba." The following quiz contains twenty multiple choice questions about the classic original filming of *Psycho*—a story Hitchcock described as "a big comedy."

1. Why does Marion steal money from her employer?
   A. She hates her work and her employer and wants to get out of a dead-end job.
   B. She needs money to move to California.
   C. She steals the money to help pay off her fiancé's debts so that they can get married.
   D. She wants the money so she can leave the country with her fiancé.

2. What type of business does Sam, Marion's fiancé, own?
   A. A hardware store   B. A service station
   C. A flower shop   D. A dry cleaners

3. What does Marion do to cover her tracks on her flight from Phoenix?
   A. She dyes her hair brown.
   B. She stops at a used car lot and buys a different car.
   C. She takes a less-traveled scenic route.
   D. She leaves Phoenix going east and then turns toward the west after she is out of the city.

4. How much money does Marion steal?
   A. $100,000   B. $40,000
   C. $25,000   D. $125,000

5. Where is Marion going when she stops at the Bates Motel?
   A. Texas   B. New Mexico
   C. Mexico   D. Southern California

6. Why is Marion forced to spend the night at the Bates Motel?
   A. A storm makes driving conditions too difficult.
   B. She is lost and decides to try and find her way in the morning.
   C. She has car trouble.
   D. She believes that she is being pursued by the police and decides to hide out in the motel.

7. What are Norman's first words to Marion?
   A. "We don't get many people down this way."
   B. "You're our only customer tonight, but we're always ready for new customers."
   C. "Dirty night."
   D. "I'm so glad you've come."

8. What is Marion's cabin number at the motel?
   A. Thirteen   B. One
   C. Seven   D. Six

9. What types of pictures decorate the walls in Marion's motel room?
   A. Pictures of circus clowns   B. Pictures of saints
   C. Pictures of Norman's mother   D. Pictures of birds

10. Where does Marion hide the money?
    A. Under the mattress
    B. In a lamp shade
    C. In the back of a dresser drawer
    D. Wrapped in a newspaper

11. What is Norman eating throughout the entire film?
    A. Peanuts   B. Candy corn
    C. Sunflower seeds   D. Popcorn

12. What is Norman's unusual hobby?
    A. He is a taxidermist with an affinity for stuffing birds.
    B. He writes bizarre poetry.
    C. He photographs corpses.
    D. He is a wood carver.

13. What painting covers Norman's peephole to the shower in Marion's room?
    A. A print of the Mona Lisa
    B. An artist's representation of the biblical character Susanna in which she is being watched while bathing
    C. A picture of Norman's mother
    D. A print of Whistler's mother

14. Where does Norman hide Marion's body?
    A. In the basement of the Bates' house
    B. Behind the motel
    C. In the trunk of her car which he pushes into a pond behind the motel
    D. In a packing trunk in the motel office under a stack of magazines

15. Who comes to the motel to investigate when Marion doesn't show up for work the next day?
    A. The local police
    B. Marion's boss and secretary
    C. Her sister, her fiancé, and an insurance investigator
    D. The same highway patrolman who stopped Marion the night before

16. What does Norman do with Arbogast's body?
    A. Buries it behind the motel
    B. Throws it into the furnace
    C. Disposes of it the same way he did Marion's
    D. Sets the body in a chair in the basement

17. What frightens Lila when she enters Mrs. Bates' bedroom?
    A. Norman is quietly rocking in his mother's chair.
    B. Her own reflection in the mirror
    C. A bird flies out of the window
    D. A cat jumps into Lila's arms

18. What is the title of the record on Norman's turntable?
    A. "Vienna Blood"
    B. "Funeral March of a Marionette"
    C. "Eroica"
    D. "Un Bel Di"

19. Who tells Lila and Sam what apparently happened to Mrs. Bates?
    A. Mr. Chambers, the sheriff   B. Mrs. Chambers
    C. Norman   D. The psychiatrist

20. What is the name of the cemetery where Mrs. Bates was supposedly buried?

A. The Meadows   B. Gracelawn

C. Memorial Park   D. Greenlawn

QUIZ 56

The Birds

UNIVERSAL (1963), COLOR, 119 MINUTES

Was it perfectionism or punishment that drove Alfred Hitchcock to subject star Tippi Hedren to a grueling ordeal while filming the final gory attack scene in *The Birds*? Hitchcock's personal obsession with his "new creation," Tippi Hedren, turned sour when she refused to succumb to his attempts to control her life both on and off the set. Hitchcock insisted that he was merely after the perfect take when the actress collapsed after a week of being attacked by live birds.

"When they started shooting, they hurled all these birds at me and I just had to fend them off," Hedren reveals. "The humane society was there the whole time, and I was wondering, where's the humane society for me?" The filming was suspended for an entire week so that the distraught Hedren could recover. The following quiz contains twelve true/false statements about the film in which Alfred Hitchcock claimed the only stars were the birds and himself.

1. When Mitch Brenner enters the pet store he mistakes Melanie for the salesclerk.

2. Mitch is a plastic surgeon.

3. Melanie follows Mitch to his apartment, notes his address, and calls a friend who works for the phone company to get Mitch's name and number.

4. The first bird attack occurs when Melanie is in the boat returning to town after leaving her gift at Mitch's weekend home.

5. The name of the local cafe, which is the setting for the panic scene, is The Crow's Nest.

6. The death of Mrs. Brenner's chickens is the first significant sign that something is amiss.

7. Mitch's mother, Lydia, disapproves of Melanie because she heard a rumor that Melanie jumped nude into a fountain while jet-setting in Europe.

8. Crows attack the children at the party.

9. Swallows fly down the Brenners' chimney and invade their house.

10. The first character to die from a bird attack is the schoolteacher, Annie Hayworth.

11. The crowd of locals at the cafe blame Melanie for the birds' attacks because they began occurring after she came to town.

12. The letters on Melanie's license plate are AVES 666.

QUIZ **57**

Marnie

UNIVERSAL (1964), COLOR, 130 MINUTES

During the making of *Marnie*, Hitchcock's escalating obsession with his twenty-nine- year-old, gorgeous leading lady, Tippi Hedren, grew into an uncontrollable desire. He choreographed Hedren's every nuance, and eventually closed the set to the public, creating a private intimacy in which he may have actually viewed himself as her leading man. The sixty-five-year-old director was quoted as saying, "Don't you understand that you're everything I've ever dreamed about? If it weren't for Alma . . ." However, the director's feelings were not reciprocated by the disinterested Ms. Hedren. She was engaged to be married after the filming, and became emotionally distraught over Hitchcock's persistence. The following quiz contains twelve short-answer questions.

1. After she robs Mr. Strutt, Marnie changes her hair color and clothes and puts her luggage in a locker. What does she do with the key?

2. What is the name of the horse Marnie rides at the stable?

3. What color triggers a state of rage in Marnie?

4. From where does Mark Rutland remember Marnie?

5. Where is the combination to the Rutland safe kept?

6. Besides the particular color, what else sends Marnie into a state of rage?

7. What was Mark's profession before he took over the family business?

8. On what subject does Mark ask Marnie to type a paper?

9. At what restaurant chain do Mark and Marnie stop and have lunch?

10. What is the cost of the engagement ring that Mark buys Marnie?

11. What does Marnie do after Mark forces himself on her during their honeymoon?

12. What tragic memory does Marnie block out?

Trivia Facts:
Did You Know That . . .

Now You See Him, Now You Don't—Anthony Perkins did not do the shower scene in *Psycho*; instead, a double was used. At the time the sequence was filmed, Perkins was in New York starring in a Broadway play.

Now You See Her, Now You Don't—Hitchcock insisted that no one be admitted into theatres after each showing of *Psycho* started because his leading lady, Janet Leigh, did not appear in the second half of the thriller.

The Return of the Birds—At the end of his film, Hitchcock deliberately eliminated the words "The End" in order to give *The Birds* an ongoing perspective.

The Midas Touch—The syndication of Hitchcock's television series in the 1960s gave him a $7 million profit.

Wealthy and Wealthier—*The Birds* brought in $11 million after the first month of release. This almost equaled the revenue from *Psycho*, which at that time had grossed an impressive $14 million.

The Object of His Obsession—After the filming of *Marnie*, Tippi Hedren was to receive the Photoplay Award on TV's *The Tonight Show* as the year's most promising new actress. Because of the strained situation between Hitchcock and Hedren, and because he didn't want her to be away, even for a few days (*The Tonight Show* was then taped in New York), Hitchcock telephoned the magazine and rejected the award on her behalf.

Put the Best Feet Forward—Hitchcock claimed that he had an ankle fetish, which explained why there were so many shots of women's ankles in his films.

QUIZ **58**

Torn Curtain

UNIVERSAL (1966), COLOR, 125 MINUTES

Against Hitchcock's wishes, Universal signed Paul Newman and Julie Andrews for his next picture. When *Torn Curtain* was released, the reviews for this bloated espionage suspense film were lukewarm at best. Hitchcock blamed its artistic failure on the lack of onscreen charisma between Newman and Andrews. "We'd have done much better with the picture without Julie Andrews or Paul Newman. Bad chemistry, that was," commented Hitchcock. "Just because they happened to be hot." The following quiz contains eight multiple choice questions.

1. What makes Sarah suspicious of Michael's behavior?
   A. She notices him making unplanned travel arrangements at the hotel.
   B. He starts making phone calls from the hotel lobby instead of his room.
   C. She follows him and discovers that he lied to her about where he was going.
   D. He suddenly becomes cranky and moody.

2. What is the symbol used to identify Michael to his allies in Germany?
   A. Ψ   B. Ω
   C. β   D. Π

3. What project has Michael been working on in the United States?
   A. A chemical weapons project
   B. A top secret biochemical weapon
   C. An antimissile project designed to eliminate nuclear weapons
   D. A project to develop a nuclear warhead

4. How is Gromek murdered?
   A. He is pushed in front of a tractor.
   B. He is skewered with a pitchfork when he runs into the barn.
   C. He is knocked unconscious, then held underwater in the cistern.
   D. He is stabbed and then asphyxiated in an oven.

5. What is the real reason Michael is in East Berlin?
   A. He wants to convince Dr. Lindt to defect to the United States in order to help him complete his project.
   B. He wants to gain the trust of Dr. Lindt in order to get information to complete his project.
   C. He intends to give Dr. Lindt false information in order to ruin the project.
   D. He plans to steal the formula from Dr. Lindt and return to the United States to complete his project.

6. Who is Michael and Sarah's ally when things go wrong and they need to escape from the university and return to Berlin?
   A. Dr. Koska   B. Dr. Lindt
   C. Dr. Lindt's lab assistant   D. Mr. Jacobi

7. What is the name of the ballet being performed when Michael and Sarah are in the audience trying to escape from the police? Hint: Michael creates a diversion by yelling, "Fire!"
   A. *Firebird*   B. *Pillar of Fire*
   C. *Dante's Inferno*   D. *Three Virgins and a Devil*

8. Once in Berlin, how are Michael and Sarah able to escape to Sweden?
   A. They travel on a tour bus from Berlin to Sweden via Denmark.
   B. A resistance movement has fake passports for them and they are able to leave the country via a commercial airliner.
   C. They stow away on a fishing boat bound for Sweden.
   D. They hide in a ballet company costume basket on a ship bound for Sweden.

QUIZ **59**

Topaz

UNIVERSAL (1969), COLOR, 126 MINUTES

Hitchcock viewed his second cold-war espionage film as a complete disaster. Three endings of this movie, dealing with political upheaval in Cuba, were shot. Hitchcock's least favorite of the three won out as the choice of Universal Pictures. The director's preference was to have had the two main characters, an American and a Russian, fight a duel in an empty stadium. Before the political enemies could kill each other the Russian would be assassinated by a sniper acting for the Soviet government. Hitchcock felt that this coup de grâce would have added a fitting sense of political justice to this cold-war drama. The following quiz contains ten true/false statements.

1. Michael Nordstrom convinces André Dévereaux to act as a liaison between the United States and Cuba to gather information on Cuba's military strategy.

2. Philippe Dubois, masquerading as a reporter for *Ebony* magazine, is able to get an interview with Rico Parra.

3. André brings Juanita de Cordoba a gift box containing a tape recorder, camera with a remote control, a Geiger counter, and a handbag.

4. The Cuban soldiers discover Juanita's spies photographing the Russian operations when the flash from their cameras gives away their location.

5. Before Carlotta is arrested she hides her camera under a loose plank on the bridge.

6. Juanita de Cordoba's espionage equipment is hidden in a secret room in the basement.

7. Juanita is the mistress of both Rico Parra and André Dévereaux.

8. André unknowingly smuggles the microfilm out of Cuba because Juanita has glued the film under the endpaper of a book she gave him.

9. Topaz is Juanita's code name.

10. Jacques Granville (code name: Columbine) is the link between the Soviet Union spy ring and the French.

CHAPTER 7

The 1970s—
The End of an Era

"One never knows the ending. One has

to die to know exactly what happens after death,

although Catholics have their hopes."

ALFRED HITCHCOCK, 1970S

ALFRED HITCHCOCK WAS ASSIDUOUSLY WORKING ON A new feature film in 1979, when he was forced to close his office on the Universal lot and "officially" end his career. The desire to finish this movie, *The Short Night*, and the need to release his inner turmoil had never been stronger in his life. Almost as a last hurrah, he dictated the opening scene with revived clarity and conviction. The sequence involves an escaped convict desperately seeking refuge in the care of a beautiful young woman. When she rejects his sexual advances, he is unable to control his rage and kills her. However, the story was never brought to fruition. Due to his frail health and excessive use of alcohol, Hitchcock was forced to abandon this final screen project and retire to his Hollywood estate.

Prior to this aborted vehicle, however, Alfred Hitchcock did complete two other films in the 1970s, both of which were successful. For the production of *Frenzy* (1972), Hitchcock returned to England and back to the neighborhood where he grew up to shoot the most harrowing, sexually explicit picture of his lengthy movie career. Hired to write the screenplay, Anthony Shaffer felt that this gruesome story (of an impotent rapist-strangler—a concept that haunted and fascinated Hitchcock throughout his career) was an inevitable project, one that Hitchcock was driven to complete. The film became a remarkable success, grossing more than $16 million. In his Hitchcock biography, *The Dark Side of Genius: The Life of Alfred Hitchcock* (1983), Donald Spoto stated, "For all its cinematic inventiveness, it remains one of the most repellent examples of a detailed murder in the history of films."

The second production, *Family Plot* (1976), was, in contrast, a light, cheerful, comic thriller. It reflected a mood rarely seen in Hitchcock's oncamera work. *Family Plot* was well received, perhaps because it offered a welcome departure from the heavy, destructive nature of his previous films.

Alfred Hitchcock spent a lifetime making his fantasies come to life on the screen. By freeing these fantasies, did he attempt to release himself of the troubles that plagued him throughout his life? When he was unable to complete *The Short Night*, did he recognize this as an omen of the approaching end of his own life's story? However, as with any ending, he continued to revise and rewrite, attempting to achieve cinematic perfection until near his last days.

QUIZ

Frenzy

UNIVERSAL (1972), COLOR, 116 MINUTES

Hitchcock took full advantage of the now-relaxed censorship standards in Hollywood when filming *Frenzy*. Because of the nudity and graphic rape scene, *Frenzy* was Hitchcock's first R-rated film. The director described his new movie as "the story of a man who is impotent and therefore expresses himself through murder." This bizarre thriller received rave reviews and was considered his most successful exploit since *Psycho*. The following quiz contains twelve short-answer questions.

1. What is the name of the horse Bob Rusk tells Dick to bet on?

2. When Dick and Babs check into the Coburg Hotel how does he sign the register?

3. How does £20 wind up in Dick's coat pocket?

4. Who calls the police from the hotel and turns Dick in?

5. How are the police able to trace the £10 note Dick used to pay for the hotel room back to his ex-wife, Brenda?

6. Why does Bob return and search for Babs after he disposes of her body?

7. Why do the police stop the potato truck?

8. What does Bob do that incriminates Dick?

9. What punishment does Dick receive for killing the women?

10. How does Dick manage to escape from prison?

11. Who suspects that Dick is not guilty of the crimes for which he is convicted?

12. What evidence proves that Bob murdered the women?

Trivia Facts:
Did You Know That . . .

Modesty Rules—Hitchcock asked actress Barbara Leigh-Hunt if she had any objection to baring her breasts for the camera during the rape scene in *Frenzy* (1972). She reminded him that her contract stated that she would not engage in a nude scene. Hitchcock, therefore, was forced to use a model for the close-up nude sequence.

You Are What You Eat—In Hitchcock's extended interviews with François Truffaut, Hitchcock explained his desire to exploit the use of food as a theme for a film. This topic was vividly evident in the film *Frenzy*. The explanation is best described in Hitchcock's own words, "I'd like to try to do an anthology on food. . . . What happens to it in various hotels; how it's fixed up and absorbed. And, gradually, the end of the film would show the sewers, the garbage being dumped out into the ocean. So there's a cycle, beginning with the gleaming fresh vegetables and ending with the mess that's poured into the sewers. Thematically, the cycle would show what people do to good things. Your theme might almost be the rottenness of humanity."

And You Shall Dine Alone—During the filming of *Frenzy*, writer Anthony Shaffer complained to Hitchcock that the same lunch was served each day to the crew—Hitchcock's favorite, a small steak and a salad. The next day Shaffer received a fifteen-course meal delivered to his table, much to his embarrassment.

A Head in the River Is Worth Many in a Crowd—Hitchcock had a replica of his head made for his cameo appearance in *Frenzy*. The head was to be attached to a dummy that would be seen floating in the Thames River. This scene was used only in the trailers. In the actual feature, Hitchcock appears in a crowd, watching as a body is pulled from the Thames River.

Censoring Granddad—Alfred Hitchcock's only child, Patricia, refused to allow her family to see *Frenzy* because of the picture's explicit violence.

You Can't Keep a Good Filmmaker Down—During the making of his last picture, *Family Plot*, Hitchcock was implanted with a pacemaker to relieve his heart problems. Even after suffering complications, Hitchcock returned to work within a few weeks.

He Outgrew Balloons and Party Hats—On Hitchcock's sixty-fifth birthday in 1964, longtime friend and agent, Lew Wasserman, threw a party at Chasen's restaurant in Beverly Hills, inviting many of Hitchcock's old friends and all of the officials at the Music Corporation of America talent agency. Hitchcock's caricature was stenciled in every slice of the birthday cake.

A Penny Saved Is a Penny Earned—Universal suggested that Hitchcock cast Liza Minnelli as the psychic in the film *Family Plot*. Not wanting to pay the enormous salary required of major stars, which would eventually reduce his own percentage of the profits, Hitchcock rejected the idea.

If It Was Good Enough for Agatha Christie—Because Hitchcock was fascinated by the act of poisoning, this modus operandi occurs in seventeen of his fifty-three films.

Straight from the Grave—Hitchcock requested that the following epitaph be inscribed on his gravestone: "This is what we do to bad little boys."

QUIZ **61**

Family Plot

UNIVERSAL (1976), COLOR, 120 MINUTES

At the age of seventy-seven, Hitchcock's energy was beginning to wane, but his zeal and imagination were as powerful as ever. For the world premiere of his PG-rated dark comedy, *Family Plot*, Hitchcock arranged for the film to be delivered in a hearse, accompanied by a choir singing a requiem while black balloons were set adrift. The following quiz contains eight true/false questions.

1. By engaging the psychic services of Blanche Tyler, Mrs. Rainbird hopes to discover why she is having reoccurring nightmares.

2. George Lumley discovers information about the deaths of Mr. and Mrs. Shoebridge from their chauffeur.

3. When George visits the cemetery he notices that Eddy's headstone is newer than Mr. and Mrs. Shoebridge's even though they apparently died the same year.

4. Arthur and Fran keep their victims in a brick vault in their garage.

5. Arthur hides the diamonds in the carved-out pieces of a chess set.

6. Maloney knows the Adamsons from the time he hired them to kill his parents.

7. Maloney tries to kill Blanche and George by running their car off the side of a cliff.

8. Eddy Shoebridge and Maloney are the same person.

CHAPTER 8

The Television Decade—
"Good Evening,
Ladies and Gentlemen"

"It [television] can be compared to the

introduction of indoor plumbing—it brought no

change in the public's habits, it simply

eliminated the necessity of leaving the house."

ALFRED HITCHCOCK, 1966

EVERYONE WHO WATCHED TELEVISION DURING THE 1950s and 1960s remembers the slow, eerie voice with an English accent that greeted viewers with: "Good evening, ladies and gentlemen." Television audiences saw more than 200 episodes in which Hitchcock stepped into that famous silhouette profile to prepare us for a healthy dose of suspense.

In the mid-1950s, television melodramas and suspense stories were becoming increasingly popular. Hitchcock's agent, Lew Wasserman, urged Hitchcock to take advantage of this new, lucrative medium. Spurred by anticipated financial success, Hitchcock signed in 1955 with the CBS network and sponsor Bristol-Myers to do a weekly half-hour series entitled *Alfred Hitchcock Presents*. The show was an immediate success, and from 1955 to 1960 the show was rated as one of the most popular TV series.

Hitchcock assembled a creative staff, many of whom had worked for him in the past, and supervised the script writing. In describing his preference for the monologue style to James Allardice, the playwright hired to write the episode introductions, Hitchcock used his film, *The Trouble with Harry* (1955), as an example of the "offbeat humor" he wished to portray. These monologues, along with Hitchcock's audacious mocking of his sponsors, created an intimate but jovial relationship between Hitchcock and his TV viewership. After all, a commercial break in the suspense was irritating to audiences even several decades ago. The sponsors initially objected to such unconventional treatment, but when their sales figures increased, Hitchcock was allowed to continue with this humorous belittling. In 1960, the show was moved to NBC and was increased to an hour's length series entitled *The Alfred Hitchcock Hour*. It returned to CBS in 1963, where production continued until 1965. As his ten years in television came to a close, Hitchcock gave the most appropriate eulogy: "*I shall mark the completion of ten years on television. That is a long time to be getting away with murder, but they seem to have caught up with me at last. I am not sure what my punishment will be, but I suspect I shall be strapped to a chair and placed in front of an open television set.*"

In 1985, twenty years later (and five years after the great director's death), the series returned to network television (NBC). Films of Hitchcock's original black-and-white introductions were colored by computer processing, thus giving Hitchcock the unique distinction of "coming back from the dead" to introduce each episode. Some of the color installments made for this 1985–86 revival series were new stories and some were remakes of scripts from the original series. Undoubtedly, Hitchcock would have enjoyed the humor entailed in his "talking from the grave" during this one-year revival run of the TV series.

QUIZ **62**

Television Plots

Hitchcock personally directed only twenty programs for his TV series. However, he filmed prologues and epilogues for each one, poking fun at the sponsors, the plot, and, at times, the audience: "You needn't sit there staring. We're not going to show you any more. In fact, I'm not even going to tell you what happened. Television audiences are becoming entirely too dependent." The following quiz contains ten plots to match with the episode titles.

EPISODE PLOT

1. A wife waits for a glacier to melt,
   Releasing her husband who's ridden with guilt;
   But frozen in ice is a secret to hide:
   A locket with his lover's picture inside.

2. A leg of lamb, frozen and stout,
   A wife who won't let her husband walk out.
   She plans a perfect murder to happen
   By feeding the detectives the murder weapon.

3. A murdered wife, buried in the basement,
   Leaves a husband free of attachment.
   But before her death, she planned a surprise
   To excavate the basement and put a wine cellar inside.

4. Not liking her boyfriend, she grows tired of his face
   And murders him soon, but leaves a wide trace.
   So along comes father to cover her trail,
   By finding an innocent neighbor to nail.

5. Conniving and greedy, he wants it all,
   And cheats his shipmates by faking a fall
   Into the ocean to emerge a winner,
   But rescue is not for the greedy sinner.

6. How does a wife explain to her spouse
   The gift of a mink given by some other louse?
   The answer, for sure, is a bogus pawn ticket,
   But the mink ends up on the husband's girlfriend (trinket).

7. A woman screams, "He's the man who attacked."
   Her husband then kills him—he simply cracked.
   But no sooner do they proceed anew
   Than she points again and says, "That's him, too."

8. David Wade's plan is clever, at best:
   He hides his wife's body, laying her to rest.
   But a patrolman stops him on that dreary night—
   David did not plan on a broken taillight.

9. A detective makes a killer tell all that he can,
   By hiring an actress to play the dead man.
   The act works, and the confession is made,
   But the actress' arrival is much too delayed.

10. His life is perfect, well-ordered and right,
    Until he is seen in *two* places one night.
    His clone is clever, adapting to the mission,
    And thus unbelieved, he is sent to prison.

EPISODE TITLE

A. "Dip in the Pool"

B. "One More Mile to Go"

C. "The Crystal Trench"

D. "Revenge"

E. "Banquo's Chair"

F. "Back for Christmas"

G. "Mrs. Bixby and the Colonel's Coat"

H. "Lamb to the Slaughter"

I. "Wet Saturday"

J. "The Case of Mr. Pelham"

QUIZ **63**

Television Actors

Hitchcock employed both veteran and inexperienced actors to play the leads in the weekly episodes of his TV series. The following quiz contains twenty episode titles and the names of twenty-two actors. Match the actor with the episode. Note: actors may appear in more than one episode and episodes may contain more than one actor.

EPISODE TITLE

1. "Breakdown" (1955)

2. "Revenge" (1955)

3. "The Case of Mr. Pelham" (1955)

4. "Premonition" (1955)

5. "Momentum" (1956)

6. "The Perfect Crime" (1957)

7. "Four O'Clock" (1957)

8. "Lamb to the Slaughter" (1958)

9. "Dip in the Pool" (1958)

10. "Human Interest Story" (1959)

11. "Arthur" (1959)

12. "Man from the South" (1960)

13. "Craig's Will" (1960)

14. "Incident at a Corner" (1960)

15. "Mrs. Bixby and the Colonel's Coat" (1960)

16. "The Horseplayer" (1961)

17. "The Right Kind of Medicine" (1961)

18. "I Saw the Whole Thing" (1962)

19. "The Dividing Wall" (1963)

20. "The Return of Verge Likens" (1964)

ACTOR

A. Vera Miles

B. John Forsythe

C. Laurence Harvey

D. Robert Redford

E. Cloris Leachman

F. Audrey Meadows

G. Aaron Spelling

H. Joseph Cotten

I. E. G. Marshall

J. Tom Ewell

K. Vincent Price

L. Dick Van Dyke

M. Katharine Ross

N. Peter Lorre

O. Barbara Bel Geddes

P. Keenan Wynn

Q. George Peppard

R. Claude Rains

S. Fay Wray

T. Peter Fonda

U. Steve McQueen

V. Joanne Woodward

CHAPTER 9

Biography— The Life and Times of Alfred Hitchcock

"They say that when a man drowns,

his entire life flashes before his eyes.

I am indeed fortunate for having

just had that same experience without

even getting my feet wet."

ALFRED HITCHCOCK, 1966

LOOKING CLOSELY AT ALFRED HITCHCOCK'S CANON OF films, one notices several early influences that later formed the matrix of his artistic genius. Guilt and fear were often used as principal themes in his motion pictures. This could have resulted from growing up in England in a strict Catholic family. His upbringing held the seed that germinated the strong desires and obsessions which became controlling factors in his adult life.

Hitchcock once related the story of how his father, with the intention of shaping young Alfred's behavior, had sent him to the police station. Alfred was only five years old at the time, but his father had given prior instructions to the attending officer to lock up his son to show him what could happen to bad little boys. As a result, Hitchcock developed a life-long fear, bordering on paranoia, of police and imprisonment. It became one of the driving forces in much of his screen and TV work.

Many of his oncamera characters were innocent people being pursued by the police and forcibly handcuffed, or imprisoned in strange surroundings. Ben McKenna/Bob Lawrence in *The Man Who Knew Too Much,* (1934 and 1956), Barry Kane in *Saboteur* (1942), and Roger Thornhill in *North by Northwest* (1959) found themselves innocent victims in harrowing situations where they are left to their own devices to escape from the nightmare inflicted upon them. However, the attempt to vicariously alleviate his own demons through his films only strengthened Hitchcock's fixation on the motif of tormenting the helpless. As time progressed, his screen characters became victims of greater tragedies, and in many cases—such as Marion Crane in *Psycho* (1960) and Brenda Blaney in *Frenzy* (1972)—their release was unattainable.

QUIZ **64**

Life on the High Road: Growing Up in London

Much of Hitchcock's childhood experiences and memories were relived in his films in plots that cast out sinful demons and exorcised personal guilt. Many of his leading characters were innocent victims who had to struggle to free themselves from entrapment, much like Hitchcock did with the experiences of his childhood. The following quiz contains six multiple choice questions about Alfred Hitchcock's childhood.

1. What prank did Hitchcock play on the priests at school?
   A. He locked the doors of the chapel from the inside, requiring the doors to be removed for entry.
   B. He stole eggs from the henhouse and threw them at the Jesuit priests.
   C. He melted candle wax on the edges of each piece of classroom chalk. When his teacher attempted to write on the blackboard, no mark was made.
   D. He pretended to sleepwalk and wandered into the priests' residence in the middle of the night, causing an uproar.

2. What was the nickname his classmates gave him when he enrolled in school?
   A. Cocky   B. Alfie
   C. Hitch   D. Dodger

3. According to Hitchcock, upon his return home every evening, what ritual developed between himself and his mother that led to his strong guilt feelings?
   A. He stood at the foot of his mother's bed while she interrogated him about his daily activities.
   B. Mrs. Hitchcock would require him to recite verbatim the lessons learned in school.
   C. Mrs. Hitchcock demanded a sort of confession, implying that he must have been up to mischief.
   D. Mrs. Hitchcock would lecture him on the Ten Commandments, selecting a particular commandment that she felt applied to his behavior.

4. Hitchcock was a loner as a child and entertained himself by inventing games. What was one childhood fascination that he enjoyed?
   A. He would take the train to an unfamiliar location in London and try to find his way home on foot.
   B. He spent hours constructing detailed models of bridges and structures.
   C. He memorized the train timetables, and rode every tramline in London.
   D. He used to hide for hours, frightening his parents.

5. Hitchcock's grocer father delivered his goods by horse cart long after motorcars came into existence. In which Hitchcock film did the director use a passing grocer's horse cart to delay the police in pursuit?
   A. *Stage Fright*   B. *Frenzy*
   C. *Saboteur*   D. *To Catch a Thief*

6. Where did young Hitchcock study criminal behavior, taking detailed notes for later reference?
   A. He studied criminal cases by reading law journals.
   B. He befriended a sergeant at the neighborhood police station.
   C. He read as many books on crime as he could get his hands on.
   D. He often visited the Old Bailey Court, watching murder trials.

QUIZ 65

Great Idea:
Influences and Inspirations

Alfred Hitchcock was inspired by stories he read as a child, articles in current magazines, vivid real-life images, and by intriguing people to whom he was attracted. The following quiz contains ten short-answer questions about the inspiration behind the genius.

1. Who inspired Hitchcock to create suspense films?

2. What novelist's detective stories did Hitchcock enjoy reading when he was a teenager?

3. What author's adventures was *The Secret Agent* based on?

4. Which film was based on a short story by famed mystery writer Cornell Woolrich in which an invalid confined to his room was eventually attacked by a man who lived across the courtyard?

5. Which movie was based on a true story that was reported in *Life* magazine in 1952, in which an innocent man was charged with an armed robbery?

6. Which film's climax was inspired by a comic strip character called "The One Note Man," a musician whose life centered around playing a single note on his flute during the symphony?

7. Where did Alfred Hitchcock get the idea for the farmer having his eyes gouged out by the birds in the film, *The Birds*?

8. What architect inspired the design for the house in South Dakota in the thriller *North by Northwest*?

9. Which film depicting two women flirting with each other was inspired by an incident in Germany when Hitchcock and his director were invited to a gay bar?

10. Between 1900 and 1920, a very popular play, *Humanity*, was believed to have inspired a scene in a Hitchcock picture in which characters smash furniture in a chapel while onlookers watch with disbelief and amusement. What was this Hitchcock production?

QUIZ **66**

Hitchcock and His Blondes

Hitchcock had a thing for blonde women—specifically cool, elegant, sophisticated blondes. He liked to put them in danger on camera, to see them lose their cool, to reduce them to emotional wrecks. He liked to expose them in films as "ladies who become whores once they're in the bedroom" (as told to interviewer François Truffaut). The first "Hitchcock blonde" was Anny Ondra, who starred in *The Manxman* and *Blackmail* (both 1929). Grace Kelly represented blonde perfection to the director, and she starred in three of his best films. Tippi Hedren was the last blonde in Hitchcock's directorial life, an association that ended in bitterness on and off camera.

The following quiz concerns fifteen blonde women to be found in Hitchcock's movies. Match the star to the role she played on film.

STAR

A. Joan Barry

B. Anne Baxter

C. Karen Black

D. Doris Day

E. Marlene Dietrich

F. Joan Fontaine

G. Tippi Hedren

H. Grace Kelly

I. Priscilla Lane

J. Janet Leigh

K. Carole Lombard

L. Vera Miles

M. Kim Novak

N. Eva Marie Saint

O. Ann Todd

ROLE

1. She finally gets to sing at Albert Hall—or is that screaming?

2. She's being blackmailed for her affair with a man who became a priest.

3. In real life, she committed the one unforgivable sin by referring to Hitchcock's weight.

4. Her black bra was just the first surprise for audiences.

5. She's sexually aroused by crime, but she's not really a blonde—that's a wig she's wearing.

6. Hitchcock saw her as his new Grace Kelly—but she thought he was becoming too friendly, and became pregnant to keep from starring in *Vertigo*.

7. "Here, hold them," says this regal blonde. "They're the most beautiful thing in the world." Yet, is she referring only to her diamonds?

8. This actress was only *heard* by the audience in one Hitchcock film— but then starred in another.

9. Hitchcock directed a rarely seen film as a friendly gesture to this actress, but had no apparent interest in it.

10. She's suspicious of a glass of milk that glows in the dark.

11. An English actress, she's best known for the three films directed by her Academy Award–winning director-husband.

12. She sings a song that became a staple of her stage/nightclub act.

13. She plays two characters in the same film, one blonde, one not.

14. She's part of a chase which climaxes with the hero battling a bad guy on a national monument.

15. Now, name another film with the same description as Number Fourteen.

CHAPTER 10

Answers

QUIZ 1

Film Plots: The Moral of the Story

1. *Rebecca*
2. *Mr. and Mrs. Smith*
3. *Rope*
4. *Suspicion*
5. *The Man Who Knew Too Much* (1934)
6. *Notorious*
7. *Foreign Correspondent*
8. *Psycho*
9. *Saboteur*
10. *Dial M for Murder*
11. *Strangers on a Train*
12. *Vertigo*
13. *The Birds*
14. *Rear Window*
15. *Shadow of a Doubt*
16. *Marnie*
17. *North by Northwest*
18. *To Catch a Thief*
19. *The Trouble with Harry*
20. *Frenzy*

QUIZ 2

Art and Technique: Dark and Stormy Nights

1. C. *Suspicion*
2. D. *Rope*
3. A. *Dial M for Murder*
4. B. *Rear Window*
5. A. *Blackmail*
6. B. *Notorious*
7. A. *Foreign Correspondent*
8. D. *Strangers on a Train*
9. D. *Murder*
10. C. *Strangers on a Train*
11. D. *Young and Innocent*
12. A. *Blackmail*
13. B. *Rope*
14. D. *Psycho*
15. B. *Rich and Strange*
16. A. *Frenzy*
17. C. *North by Northwest*
18. D. *Under Capricorn*
19. A. *Dial M for Murder*
20. B. *The Lodger*

QUIZ 3

The Cameo: Hitchcock's Signature

1. O. *Young and Innocent*
2. R. *Strangers on a Train*
3. Q. *The Man Who Knew Too Much* (1956)
4. B. *The Paradine Case*
5. N. *Psycho*
6. K. *The Lady Vanishes*
7. S. *The Lodger*
8. W. *Family Plot*
9. C. *The Birds*
10. H. *Spellbound*
11. X. *North by Northwest*
12. D. *Notorious*
13. J. *Rebecca*
14. M. *Dial M for Murder*
15. A. *Rear Window*
16. U. *Topaz*
17. T. *Blackmail*
18. Y. *To Catch a Thief*
19. F. *Lifeboat*
20. P. *Stage Fright*
21. L. *Under Capricorn*
22. E. *The 39 Steps*
23. I. *Frenzy*
24. G. *Shadow of a Doubt*
25. V. *Torn Curtain*

QUIZ 4

Hitchcock Quotes: Candid and Coy

1. E. *Jamaica Inn*
2. N. *Mr. and Mrs. Smith*
3. P. *Rear Window*
4. H. *Psycho*
5. D. *Rebecca*
6. K. *The Trouble with Harry*
7. J. *The Birds*
8. Q. *Under Capricorn*
9. F. *Vertigo*
10. M. *Juno and the Paycock*
11. O. *Stage Fright*
12. G. *Number Seventeen*
13. R. *Easy Virtue*
14. B. *North by Northwest*
15. H. *Psycho*
16. L. *Strangers on a Train*
17. C. *Spellbound*
18. I. *Dial M for Murder*
19. T. *The Man Who Knew Too Much* (1956)
20. S. *Rope*

QUIZ 5

Landmarks: And If You Look to Your Left . . .

1. H. *The Man Who Knew Too Much* (1956)
2. E. *North by Northwest*
3. D. *Blackmail*
4. M. *Saboteur*
5. C. *The Paradine Case*
6. N. *Frenzy*
7. A. *Strangers on a Train*
8. G. *Family Plot*
9. E. *North by Northwest*

10. K. *To Catch a Thief*
11. B. *The Manxman*
12. J. *Topaz*

13. L. *Sabotage*
14. F. *Vertigo*
15. I. *Torn Curtain*

QUIZ 6

Awards and Achievements: And the Winner Is . . .

1. B. *Rear Window*
2. C. Edgar for *Rear Window*
3. D. Best Television Series of the Year
4. A. *North by Northwest*
5. B. *Rebecca* and *To Catch a Thief*
6. B. *Rebecca*
7. C. Five: *Rebecca* (1940), *Lifeboat* (1944), *Spellbound* (1945), *Rear Window* (1954), and *Psycho* (1960)
8. D. New York Film Critics
9. B. Columbia University
10. B. *Frenzy*
11. A. 1968
12. A. University of California at Santa Cruz
13. C. Special Editors Award
14. D. Princess Anne
15. B. Boston
16. B. American Film Institute
17. A. Man of the Year
18. D. 1980
19. D. Grace Kelly
20. C. Screen Producers Guild

QUIZ 7

Character Profiles: The Good, the Bad, and the Scary

1. John Aysgarth in *Suspicion*
2. Lisa Carol Freemont in *Rear Window*
3. Kate Caesar in *The Manxman*
4. Ann Smith in *Mr. and Mrs. Smith*
5. Elsa Carrington in *The Secret Agent*
6. John Ferguson in *Vertigo*
7. L. B. Jeffries in *Rear Window*
8. Roger Thornhill in *North by Northwest*
9. Marnie Edgar in *Marnie*
10. Manny Balestrero in *The Wrong Man*
11. Norman Bates in *Psycho*
12. Bruno Anthony in *Strangers on a Train*
13. Frances Stevens in *To Catch a Thief*
14. Constance Porter in *Lifeboat*
15. Charlie Newton in *Shadow of a Doubt*

QUIZ 8

Casting: Lead and Supporting Roles

1. Q. Cary Grant
2. CC. Kim Novak
3. JJ. Joel McCrea
4. J. James Stewart

5. QQ. Tallulah Bankhead
6. VV. Robert Walker
7. Y. Rod Taylor
8. N. Doris Day

9. DD. Madeleine Carroll
10. AAA. Joseph Cotton
11. A. Paul Newman
12. I. Anthony Perkins
13. Q. Cary Grant
14. KK. Robert Cummings
15. U. Laurence Olivier
16. S. Ingrid Bergman
17. Q. Cary Grant
18. EEE. Shirley MacLaine
19. WW. Ray Milland
20. E. Henry Fonda
21. DDD. Bruce Dern
22. RR. Leslie Banks
23. LL. Anny Ondra
24. B. Peter Lorre
25. Q. Cary Grant
26. V. Gregory Peck
27. W. William Bendix
28. K. Eva Marie Saint
29. L. Grace Kelly
30. GGG. Janet Leigh
31. FF. Barry Foster
32. O. Tippi Hedren
33. S. Ingrid Bergman
34. D. Joan Fontaine
35. X. Charles Laughton
36. MM. Carole Lombard
37. V. Gregory Peck
38. XX. Anne Baxter
39. L. Grace Kelly
40. SS. Farley Granger
41. P. Raymond Burr
42. D. Joan Fontaine

43. EE. Nova Pilbeam
44. AA. Marlene Dietrich
45. O. Tippi Hedren
46. YY. John Forsythe
47. G. Sean Connery
48. L. Grace Kelly
49. HH. Robert Montgomery
50. FFF. Margaret Lockwood
51. TT. Edmund Gwenn
52. BBB. Carl Brisson
53. NN. Joan Barry
54. M. John Dall
55. J. James Stewart
56. GG. Montgomery Clift
57. KK. Robert Cummings
58. TT. Edmund Gwenn
59. Z. Barbara Bel Geddes
60. OO. Jessica Tandy
61. H. Julie Andrews
62. F. Karen Black
63. C. Vera Miles
64. R. Patricia Hitchcock
65. UU. George Sanders
66. PP. Nigel Bruce
67. BB. Martin Balsam
68. CCC. Anna Massey
69. II. James Mason
70. ZZ. Claude Rains
71. B. Peter Lorre
72. AAA. Joseph Cotten
73. T. Jerry Mathers
74. R. Patricia Hitchcock
75. HHH. Suzanne Pleshette

QUIZ 9

Offstage: Facts behind the Filming

1. True
2. False—The ending was reshot because the audience laughed at what was supposed to be a serious scene.
3. False—Hitchcock felt Burt Lancaster would have been better in the role.

4. False—Gary Cooper turned down the lead because he refused to act in a thriller.
5. True
6. False—Tippi Hedren suffered a breakdown after having live birds thrown at her for hours at a time over a period of a week.
7. True
8. False—Hitchcock did not want to cast stars for the filming of *Family Plot* because he did not wish to pay their huge salaries, which would have diminished his own percentage in the movie.
9. True
10. True
11. False—Hitchcock's first choice for the role of David Smith was Cary Grant.
12. False—Emma was modeled after Hitchcock's mother.
13. False—The original title for *Shadow of a Doubt* was *Uncle Charlie*.
14. False—The Hitchcock marriage proposal was written into the script for the movie *Foreign Correspondent*.
15. True

QUIZ 10
Remakes: Timeless Themes

1. B. The main characters in *Once You Meet a Stranger* were women: actresses Theresa Russell played Margo Anthony and Jacqueline Bisset appeared as Shelia Gaines.
2. C. Emily Taylor (Gwyneth Paltrow) stabs her attacker in the throat with a meat thermometer.
3. D. *Psycho*
4. A. *Rear Window*
5. C. *Obsession*
6. D. *Shadow of a Doubt*
7. B. *The Man Who Knew Too Much* (1956)
8. B. *Vertigo*
9. A. *Notorious*
10. D. *Dressed to Kill*

QUIZ 11
The Pleasure Garden (1925)

1. B. Her friend Patsy arranges for Jill to work at the theatre.
2. A. Hugh is in the service and is transferred.
3. B. Levett is living with a native woman.
4. B. Levett loses his mind and tries to kill Patsy.
5. C. A local doctor

QUIZ 12
The Lodger: A Story of the London Fog (1926)

1. A triangular piece of paper with the word "Avenger" written on it.
2. The serial killer always strikes on Tuesdays.
3. The lodger demands that the pictures of blonde young women be removed from the walls.
4. The black bag contains a map marking the murder locations, newspaper clippings of the murder victims, and a picture of a woman.
5. The real killer is caught.

QUIZ 13
Downhill (1927)

1. False—The title symbolizes the social demise of a person's respectability.
2. True
3. False—Roddy goes to Paris.
4. False—Roddy becomes a professional dancer.
5. False—Roddy returns home to find that his parents have learned of his innocence and are sorry for their actions.

QUIZ 14
Easy Virtue (1927)

1. A. Larita and John meet on the Mediterranean in the south of France.
2. A. John's family does not approve of his new wife because they know nothing about her.
3. B. John's sister finds an old newspaper with the story of Larita's divorce.
4. D. John doubts her love and eventually rejects Larita.
5. D. "Shoot! There's nothing left to kill."

QUIZ 15
The Ring (1927)

1. Jack is fighting for his wife.
2. Nellie is out with Bob.
3. Nellie uses her photograph of Bob.
4. Jack is almost knocked out.
5. "I'm in your corner."

QUIZ 16
The Farmer's Wife (1928)

1. False—Mrs. Sweetland's last words are, "and don't forget to air your master's pants, Minta."
2. False—She turns down Samuel's proposal because she is too independent to marry.
3. True
4. True
5. False—Samuel scratches all the names off his list of prospective wives and writes Minta's name at the top.

QUIZ 17
Champagne (1928)

1. B. The title comes from the fact that Betty's father is in the champagne industry.
2. D. Betty's father tells her his stock has fallen and they are ruined financially.
3. C. Betty becomes angry because she believes he is trying to rescue her.
4. A. The older gentleman offers to be her friend and Betty decides to go with him to America.
5. B. Betty's father tells her his first message to her was a lie.

QUIZ 18
The Manxman (1929)

1. Pete goes to Africa to seek his fortune.
2. "Philip, we're free."
3. Kate turns to Philip after she leaves Pete.
4. Kate tells Philip to choose between her and his career.
5. Kate tries to kill herself by jumping off the pier.

QUIZ 19
Blackmail (1929)

1. False—The artist convinces Alice to pose in a ballet costume.
2. True
3. True
4. False—The word "knife" is used repeatedly during the meal.
5. True

QUIZ 20

Juno and the Paycock (1930)

1. C. Captain Boyle claims he has bad legs.
2. A. The Boyles inherit money from a cousin.
3. D. Joxer often speaks in verse.
4. B. A gramophone and record.
5. D. Juno and Mary go to live with Juno's sister.

QUIZ 21

Murder! (1930)

1. Diana is accused of killing her friend.
2. A juror
3. Seven guilty, three not guilty, and two undecided (both of which later switch to guilty).
4. By inviting the killer to read a part in a play
5. He dresses as a woman and as a policeman.

QUIZ 22

The Skin Game (1931)

1. True
2. False—Mr. Hornblower tells Mr. Hillcrist that if he treats him like a peer, the factories will not be built.
3. True
4. False—When her secret is revealed, Chloe tries to drown herself.
5. False—The film ends with a tree being cut down in one of the meadows.

QUIZ 23

Rich and Strange (1932)

1. B. He wants Fred and Emily to experience life by traveling around the world.
2. A. Emily meets Commander Gordon on the deck while Fred is in their cabin being seasick.
3. C. The Princess accidentally hits Fred in the eye with a puck.
4. B. Fred gives the money to the Princess.
5. C. Fred and Emily are afraid that they are going to die when the ship begins to sink.

QUIZ 24
Number Seventeen (1932)

1. Someone named Sheudrake
2. Cats scatter every time a shot is heard.
3. The young girl falls through the roof and lands in front of the detective.
4. The diamond necklace is hidden in the tank of the toilet.
5. Ben, the bum, is wearing the necklace.

QUIZ 25
The Man Who Knew Too Much (1934)

1. B. Skeet shooting
2. A. A sniper shoots and kills Bernard.
3. D. Hidden in a shaving brush
4. C. "Say nothing of what you found or you will never see your child again."
5. A. A foreign diplomat in London is to be assassinated.
6. C. Mrs. Lawrence shoots Betty's pursuer as he chases her across the roof.

QUIZ 26
The 39 Steps (1935)

1. False—His name is "Mr. Memory."
2. False—He is missing the tip of his little finger.
3. False—A hymnbook stops the bullet.
4. True
5. False—Richard and Pamela hide behind a waterfall.
6. False—The film begins and ends in a theatre.

QUIZ 27
Secret Agent (1936)

1. The film opens at a wake.
2. Richard Ashenden
3. Edgar Brodie was a writer.
4. Elsa Carrington plays Brodie's wife.
5. A button matching the one on Mr. Caypor's jacket is found near the body of a murdered British agent.
6. The American, Robert Marvin

QUIZ 28
Sabotage (1936)

1. C. A theatre and pet store
2. B. LONDON MUST NOT LAUGH ON SATURDAY.
3. D. The bomb is delivered in a bird cage with the message, "Don't forget—the birds will sing at 1:45."
4. C. Stevie is distracted by a street hawker and a parade.
5. A. *Who Killed Cock Robin?*
6. D. Lord Mayor's Show Day

QUIZ 29
Young and Innocent (1937)

1. True
2. False—Robert is a screenwriter.
3. False—Robert and Christine knew one another from when they worked together in America.
4. True
5. True
6. False—Will recognizes the murderer by his twitching eyes.

QUIZ 30
The Lady Vanishes (1938)

1. Iris and Miss Froy meet in the hotel hallway when they come out of their rooms at the same time to investigate a noise coming from the floor above.
2. A flower pot from a window ledge had dropped on her head.
3. Because of the train's noise, Miss Froy writes her name in the dust on the window.
4. When he sees the empty tea wrapper thrown away in the garbage.
5. Miss Froy hums a tune, which is the code for the message.
6. Miss Froy

QUIZ 31
Jamaica Inn (1939)

1. C. The smugglers cover the beacon, causing the ships to wreck on the rocky shores.
2. B. Mary's mother died and she is coming to live with her aunt.

3. C. Mary reaches through a hole in the floor of her second story room and cuts the rope which is attached to the rafters and to Jim's neck.
4. B. Jem is an officer of the Royal Navy sent to investigate the shipwrecks.
5. D. Patience
6. C. Sir Humphrey

QUIZ 32

Rebecca (1940)

1. D. At a hotel in Monte Carlo
2. B. The weather turns foul and it begins to rain.
3. D. Rebecca's room is the only one in the house that faces the sea.
4. B. Mrs. de Winter follows the dog to the cottage.
5. B. It is the same costume Rebecca wore to the ball before she died.
6. D. Mrs. Danvers suggests that she wear the costume because it is Maxim's favorite.
7. B. Rebecca told him she was pregnant with another man's child and Manderley would not be inherited by another de Winter.
8. A. A boat builder testifies that the seacocks on her boat were opened, indicating that the boat had been intentionally sunk.
9. A. Jack Favell, Rebecca's lover
10. C. Rebecca was dying and had only a short while to live.

QUIZ 33

Foreign Correspondent (1940)

1. Huntley Haverstock
2. Mr. Fisher
3. The assassin pretends to take Mr. Van Meer's picture, but shoots him in the face instead.
4. John keeps losing his hat.
5. Carol Fisher's father
6. John is pushed in front of a lorry.
7. The bodyguard tries to push John from a church bell tower.
8. John narrates the story to the captain of the rescue ship. The captain, who forbade that the story be leaked to the press, does not realize that John's newspaper editor is on the phone and the receiver is hidden on a shelf behind John. Everything John says is heard by his eavesdropping editor.

QUIZ 34
Mr. and Mrs. Smith (1941)

1. False—David and Ann barricade themselves in their apartment until they stop quarreling.
2. True
3. False—David stays at his club, The Beefeaters.
4. True
5. False—Ann and Jeff go to Lake Placid for the weekend to ski.

QUIZ 35
Suspicion (1941)

1. C. A book about child psychology
2. D. Lina overhears her parents discussing her grim future as a spinster.
3. A. Monkey face
4. D. Two museum-piece chairs
5. B. Johnny steals the money from his employer.
6. A. Murder
7. C. Johnny and Beaky are negotiating a real estate development venture.
8. C. A yearly inheritance of £500 and his portrait

QUIZ 36
Saboteur (1942)

1. Barry and Fry run into each other as they are leaving the factory, and Barry notices Fry's name on the envelope he drops.
2. Barry is the suspect in the sabotage of the factory.
3. Barry is traveling on Highway 395.
4. Barry realizes that Mr. Tobin is lying about not knowing Fry when Tobin's granddaughter pulls from Tobin's pocket envelopes with Fry's name on them.
5. Barry and Pat meet when Barry takes refuge at her grandfather's cabin.
6. Esmeralda, the bearded lady
7. The ship, the U.S.S. *Alaska*
8. Pat writes "SOS" on a large piece of cardboard in lipstick and throws it out the window.

QUIZ 37
Shadow of a Doubt (1943)

1. True
2. False—Uncle Charlie brings his niece an emerald ring.
3. False—Charlie is suspicious of the gift because of the engraving on the inside.
4. True
5. False—Charlie takes the newspaper and makes a paper hat for Ann, his younger niece, removing the incriminating pages.
6. True
7. False—Charlie Oakley deposits $40,000 in the bank.
8. True
9. True
10. False—Charlie Oakley falls from a train and is killed.

QUIZ 38
Lifeboat (1944)

1. *The New Yorker*
2. Rittenhouse starts the prayer, and when he can't remember it, Joe continues the eulogy.
3. Stanly ("Sparks") is in charge of navigation; Joe, the commissary; Connie, the log; Alice, sick bay.
4. Kovak uses Connie's memo pad to make a deck of cards.
5. Kovak has four tattoos on his chest and one on his arm.
6. Willi turns out to be the captain of the German ship and a surgeon.
7. Gus becomes delirious, and Willi convinces Gus to jump overboard and swim to his girlfriend.
8. Connie and Kovak both grew up on the South Side of Chicago.
9. Willi hides water, food tablets, and energy pills under his shirt.
10. Her diamond bracelet

QUIZ 39
Spellbound (1945)

1. B. Green Manors
2. C. *The Labyrinth of the Guilt Complex*
3. D. Dark parallel lines drawn on a white background
4. B. Constance notices that the signature on John's note does not match the signature in Dr. Edwardes' book.

5. B. Dr. Brulov places a drug in John's milk.
6. A. John accidentally killed his brother.
7. D. John says that Dr. Edwardes had a fatal accident while they were skiing.
8. A. Constance analyzes John's bizarre dream.

QUIZ 40
Notorious (1946)

1. False—Alicia and Alexander meet at a riding club in Rio de Janeiro.
2. False—Devlin pretends that he is no longer in love with Alicia, so she reacts by marrying Alexander.
3. True
4. False—Alicia passes Devlin the key when she shakes his hand.
5. False—The metal is uranium.
6. True
7. True
8. False—Alexander's mother decides that Alicia should die.

QUIZ 41
The Paradine Case (1947)

1. Maddalena Paradine is arrested for murdering her husband.
2. Mr. Paradine is blind.
3. The poison is placed in a glass of burgundy.
4. Mr. Keane tries to prove that André Latour murdered Mr. Paradine.
5. André Latour commits suicide during the trial.

QUIZ 42
Rope (1948)

1. True
2. False—Rupert used to be the housemaster at the prep school that Philip and Brandon attended.
3. False—Rupert is now a publisher of philosophy books.
4. False—Philip is a pianist.
5. False—Mrs. Atwell predicts that Philip's hands will bring him great fame.
6. False—Janet works for *Allure*.
7. False—They are discussing Nietzsche.
8. False—Brandon's excuse for moving the dinner party to the living room is to make Mr. Kentley more comfortable while he looks at books on the dining room table.

9. False—Rupert realizes that Philip and Brandon are lying about David when Rupert is given David's hat by mistake.
10. True

QUIZ 43
Under Capricorn (1949)

1. C. Sam wants to buy the land for himself, but he has already purchased his allotted amount.
2. B. Sam served time in prison.
3. C. Lady Henrietta is drunk and barefooted.
4. B. Charles' sister and Lady Henrietta were friends when they lived in Ireland.
5. B. Lady Henrietta goes into the kitchen and attempts to give the orders for the day.
6. B. Milly leaves out of frustration because of Lady Henrietta's newfound power.
7. A. Charles forges their names on an invitation.
8. C. Lady Henrietta killed him.
9. D. Sam shoots Charles by accident when Charles tries to take the gun away from him.
10. A.Lady Henrietta sees Milly put the shrunken head in its box and then pour all of the sleeping medication into Lady Henrietta's drink.

QUIZ 44
Stage Fright (1950)

1. False—Charlotte pleads with Johnny to return to the scene of the crime to get a clean dress because hers is covered with blood.
2. False—Charlotte's housekeeper identifies Johnny.
3. True
4. True
5. False—Eve's first role was as the fourth deadly sin in a church play.
6. False—Eva convinces Nellie to allow her to work as Charlotte's maid by telling Nellie that she is a reporter and is investigating the crime.
7. True
8. False—Inspector Smith wants Eve to call him Ordinary Smith.
9. False—Eve's father suggests that Eve hide a microphone in her clothes so that Inspector Smith can overhear Charlotte's confession.
10. False—Because she knows that he has killed once before, Charlotte believes that she can easily talk Johnny into killing again.

QUIZ 45
Strangers on a Train (1951)

1. C. Bruno drove a car 150 miles per hour while blindfolded.
2. A. Bruno plans to make reservations on the first rocket ship to the moon.
3. C. Bruno helps a blind man cross the street.
4. C. 9:20–9:25 P.M.
5. A. Miriam's glasses
6. C. Bruno's tie clip has his name engraved on it.
7. D. Miriam
8. D. A key to Bruno's house, a map of the inside of the house, and, in a second delivery, a gun
9. A. Guy wants to tell Bruno's father what Bruno has done.
10. C. Barbara bumps into the policeman, spilling the powder from her compact all over his pants.
11. D. On the carousel
12. A. A man who works at the carnival

QUIZ 46
I Confess (1953)

1. Otto Keller wants to steal $2,000 to start a new life. He feels ashamed because his wife has to work hard.
2. There is still $500 left in a cashbox in Villette's study.
3. Two schoolgirls say they saw a priest leaving Villette's house at the time of the murder, and Father Logan is the only priest who cannot, or will not, account for his time when the murder was committed.
4. Father Logan volunteered for military service and left to fight in the war.
5. The coroner says the murder was committed after 11:30 P.M., which gave Father Logan enough time to kill Villette after he returned from his rendezvous with Ruth.
6. Villette is involved in a scandal and wants Ruth's husband's help, because he is a member of Parliament and has connections.
7. Villette threatens to tell Mr. Grandfort that he has found Ruth and Father Logan together in his summer house.
8. Keller puts his bloody cassock, which he wore when he killed Villette, in Father Logan's trunk.
9. Inspector Larrue bluffs Keller into confessing by making him think that Father Logan has already told him about Keller's confession.
10. Both Mr. and Mrs. Keller say, "Forgive me," before they die.

QUIZ 47
Dial M for Murder (1954)

1. True
2. False—Tony persuades Swan to come to his apartment by pretending that he wants to buy a car that Swan is selling.
3. True
4. True
5. False—The murder is to take place at 11:00 P.M.
6. True
7. True
8. False—The murder is set up to look like an interrupted burglary.
9. False—Margot stabs Swan with a pair of scissors.
10. False—In order to compare Mark's handwriting, Inspector Hubbard asks Mark to write down his address.
11. False—Margot is given the death sentence.
12. True

QUIZ 48
Rear Window (1954)

1. B. Jeffries was taking pictures at an auto race and a race car spun out of control and careened into the press stand.
2. C. "Here lie the broken bones of L. B. Jeffries."
3. A. 21
4. A. Three—two times in the middle of the night and once the next morning
5. D. Costume jewelry
6. A. Mrs. Thorwald's clothes
7. C. When the owner finds her pet dead in the garden, all the neighbors, except Thorwald, respond to her scream.
8. A. Lisa becomes suspicious of Thorwald when she realizes Thorwald's wife did not take her favorite handbag or jewelry with her when she left.
9. B. "What have you done with her?"
10. D. Jeffries will set off a flashbulb on his camera.
11. C. Miss Lonelyhearts is about to take an overdose of pills.
12. D. "What do you want from me?"
13. D. Jeffries sets off flashbulbs in Thorwald's eyes trying to blind him.
14. D. Mrs. Thorwald's head
15. C. Lisa is reading a book entitled *Beyond the High Himalayas.*

QUIZ 49
To Catch a Thief (1955)

1. True
2. False—John gained his skill from being a trapeze artist in the circus.
3. False—John contacts Lloyd's agent with the plan to catch the copycat burglar.
4. False—John tells Mrs. Stevens and Frances that he is from Portland, Oregon, and that he is in the lumber business.
5. True
6. True
7. False—John knows where the next burglary is to take place because the thief left a smudged fingerprint on a list of potential burglary sites.
8. True

QUIZ 50
The Trouble with Harry (1955)

1. Three
2. A tramp
3. Sam cuts his cigarette packs in half and smokes one half a cigarette at a time.
4. Sam is sketching in the meadow when he notices the body.
5. Arnie asks Sam, "How did rabbits get to be born?"
6. Jennifer left Harry because he followed astrology too closely; this obsession caused him to stand her up on their wedding night.
7. The Captain accounts for all three bullets he fired earlier and wants to be sure that he did not shoot Harry and someone else killed him.
8. Miss Graveley confesses to hitting Harry over the head with her cleated hiking shoe when he mistook her for Jennifer and tried to drag her into the bushes.
9. They decide to bury Harry again to save Jennifer from being involved in a potential scandal.
10. In the bathtub
11. Sam trades his paintings for two boxes of fresh strawberries to be delivered on the first of every month for Jennifer, a smelly chemistry set for Arnie, a chromium plated cash register with a bell for Mrs. Wiggs, a hope chest for Miss Graveley, a good shotgun with ammunition, corduroy britches, a clean shirt, a brown hunting cap for the Captain, and a double bed for himself and his future bride.
12. Harry died from a heart attack.

QUIZ 51
The Man Who Knew Too Much (1956)

1. D. Marrakech, Morocco
2. A. Ben and Jo meet Bernard on a bus.
3. B. Jo was a singer.
4. D. Bernard is wearing an Arab robe and dark makeup.
5. B. Ben receives a call from the kidnappers while he is at the police station.
6. C. Ben gives Jo a sedative before he tells her the bad news.
7. B. A friend mentions that Ben is searching for a man named Church. Upon hearing the word "church," Jo realizes that Ambrose Chapel is a church, not a person.
8. C. Jo calls the police station to ask for Mr. Buchannan's help and is told that he is attending a concert at Albert Hall.
9. A. Ben climbs the rope attached to the church bell.
10. C. Jo screams and distracts the audience, causing the assassin to miss his opportunity to fire the fatal shot.
11. D. *Que Será, Será.*
12. B. Mrs. Drayton tells Hank to whistle the same song that his mother is singing.

QUIZ 52
The Wrong Man (1957)

1. False—Manny plays the bass.
2. True
3. True
4. True
5. False—The police make Manny walk into each of the stores that was robbed so that the store clerks can get a good look at him.
6. False—They go to the country house looking for a possible witness.
7. True
8. False—Rose feels intense guilt over Manny's unfortunate experience and cannot deal with her emotions.

QUIZ 53
Vertigo (1958)

1. Elster says that he is afraid that harm will come to his wife in a mysterious manner.
2. Elster insinuates that a ghost has possessed Madeleine.
3. Carlotta Valdes' grave

4. "Portrait of Carlotta"
5. The Argosy
6. To an old Spanish mission south of San Francisco
7. The jury rules that Madeleine committed suicide.
8. Scottie has a breakdown and spends several months in an institution.
9. Scottie notices Judy at the flower shop Madeleine used to visit.
10. Scottie wants Judy to dye and style her hair and to wear the same style clothes as Madeleine did.
11. Scottie realizes that Madeleine and Judy are the same person when Judy puts on Carlotta's necklace, which Madeleine inherited.
12. A nun appears in the tower and frightens Judy, causing her to fall to her death.

QUIZ 54

North by Northwest (1959)

1. B. Roger is an advertising executive.
2. C. Roger raises his hand for the waiter to bring him a phone at the same time George Kaplan is being paged.
3. A. They force him to swallow large amounts of bourbon and then try to push his car over a cliff.
4. C. A woman claiming to be Mrs. Townsend says that Roger attended her party the previous night and that he was too drunk to drive home.
5. A. Roger finds Lester Townsend at the United Nations.
6. B. After he is stabbed, Townsend falls into Roger's arms, and Roger unthinkingly pulls out the knife.
7. C. They meet on the train when Roger ducks into her compartment, trying to avoid the police.
8. B. He is fleeing the police because he has overdue parking tickets.
9. A. Eve bribes the maitre d' to seat Roger at her table.
10. C. Nothing
11. B. Roger stops a gasoline truck, causing the plane to fly into it and explode.
12. A. Using a pencil, Roger shades over the address Eve wrote on the telephone pad.
13. D. He doesn't exist.
14. B. Roger writes a note on the inside of his matchbook and throws it over the balcony to where she is sitting in the living room.
15. D. The housekeeper sees Roger's reflection in the television screen.
16. A. Roger proposes to Eve by calling her Mrs. Thornhill.

QUIZ 55
Psycho (1960)

1. C. Marion steals the money to help pay off her fiancé's debts so they can get married.
2. A. A hardware store
3. B. Marion stops at a used car lot and buys a different car.
4. B. $40,000
5. D. Southern California
6. A. A storm makes driving conditions too difficult.
7. C. "Dirty night"
8. B. One
9. D. Pictures of birds
10. D. She wraps the money in a newspaper.
11. B. Candy corn
12. A. Norman is a taxidermist with an affinity for stuffing birds.
13. B. An artist's representation of the biblical character Susanna in which she is being watched while bathing.
14. C. Norman puts her body in the trunk of her car and pushes the car into a pond behind the motel.
15. C. Marion's sister, Marion's fiancé, and an insurance investigator
16. C. Norman disposes of Arbogast's body the same way he did Marion's.
17. B. Lila jumps when she sees her own reflection in the mirror.
18. C. "Eroica"
19. B. Mrs. Chambers
20. D. Greenlawn

QUIZ 56
The Birds (1963)

1. True
2. False—Mitch Brenner is a defense attorney.
3. False—Melanie calls Charlie, one of her father's associates, and gives Charlie the license plate number of Mitch's car along with instructions to find out the name of the man who owns the vehicle.
4. True
5. False—The name of the cafe is Tides Cafe.
6. False—The first sign of trouble is when Mrs. Brenner's chickens refuse to eat.
7. True
8. False—Gulls attack the children at the party.
9. False—Sparrows fly down the Brenners' chimney.
10. False—The Brenners' neighbor, Dan Fawcett, is the first to die.

11. True
12. False—The letters on Melanie's license plate are RUJ, symbolizing the pun "Are you jay."

QUIZ 57
Marnie (1964)

1. Marnie drops the key down a grate in the street.
2. Forio
3. Red
4. Mark visited Strutt's office when Marnie worked for him.
5. The combination is taped to the inside of the top drawer of the secretary's desk.
6. Thunderstorms
7. A zoologist
8. Predators
9. Howard Johnson's
10. $42,000
11. Marnie tries to drown herself in the swimming pool.
12. Marnie killed one of her mother's lovers when he tried to attack Marnie's mother.

QUIZ 58
Torn Curtain (1966)

1. A. Sarah notices Michael making unplanned travel arrangements at the hotel.
2. D. Π
3. C. An antimissile project designed to eliminate nuclear weapons
4. D. Gromek is stabbed and then asphyxiated in an oven.
5. B. Michael wants to gain the trust of Dr. Lindt in order to get information to complete his project.
6. A. Dr. Koska
7. C. Dante's Inferno (which takes place in Hell with flames surrounding the fated lovers Paolo and Francesca)
8. D. Michael and Sarah hide in a ballet company costume basket on a ship bound for Sweden.

QUIZ 59
Topaz (1969)

1. True
2. True

3. True
4. False—The spies are discovered when a flock of noisy gulls attract the attention of the soldiers.
5. False—Carlotta hides the camera in the railing on the bridge.
6. False—Juanita's secret room is behind a wall in her pantry.
7. True
8. True
9. False—Topaz is the code name of a Communist spy ring.
10. True

QUIZ 60

Frenzy (1972)

1. Coming Up
2. Mr. and Mrs. Oscar Wilde
3. Brenda slips the money into Dick's pocket without his knowing it.
4. The porter who sends Dick's clothes to the cleaners
5. The £10 note contains face powder that matches the type Brenda wore and carried in her handbag.
6. Bob realizes that he lost his rhinestone tie pin inscribed with his initials, and fears that it was with the body in the potato sack.
7. The police stop the truck because the tailgate is left open and potatoes are spilling out on the road.
8. Bob puts Babs' clothes in Dick's bag.
9. Dick is found guilty and receives a life sentence.
10. Dick purposely trips and falls down the stairs. He is taken to a prison hospital where he later drugs the guard and escapes.
11. Inspector Oxford believes that Dick is telling the truth when he claims he is innocent. The inspector also suspects that Bob Rusk is the real killer.
12. After driving the potato truck, Bob stops at a cafe and asks for a clothes brush. A suspicious waitress turns the brush over to the police. The brush is analyzed, and the police discover that it contains potato dust.

QUIZ 61

Family Plot (1976)

1. False—Mrs. Rainbird hires Blanche to find her nephew.
2. False—George receives his information from the chauffeur's daughter.
3. True
4. True
5. False—Arthur hides the diamonds in the crystal chandelier that hangs in his foyer.

6. True
7. False—Maloney tampers with the brakes on George's car.
8. False—Eddy Shoebridge and Arthur Adamson are the same person.

QUIZ 62
Television Plots

1. C. "The Crystal Trench"
2. H. "Lamb to the Slaughter"
3. F. "Back for Christmas"
4. I. "Wet Saturday"
5. A. "Dip in the Pool"

6. G. "Mrs. Bixby and the Colonel's Coat"
7. D. "Revenge"
8. B. "One More Mile to Go"
9. E. "Banquo's Chair"
10. J. "The Case of Mr. Pelham"

QUIZ 63
Television Actors

1. H. & G. Joseph Cotten and Aaron Spelling
2. A. Vera Miles
3. J. Tom Ewell
4. E. Cloris Leachman
5. V. Joanne Woodward
6. K. Vincent Price
7. I. E. G. Marshall
8. O. Barbara Bel Geddes
9. P. & S. Keenan Wynn and Fay Wray
10. U. Steve McQueen

11. C. Laurence Harvey
12. N. Peter Lorre
13. L. Dick Van Dyke
14. A. & Q. Vera Miles and George Peppard
15. F. Audrey Meadows
16. R. Claude Rains
17. D. Robert Redford
18. B. John Forsythe
19. M. Katharine Ross
20. T. Peter Fonda

QUIZ 64
Life on the High Road: Growing Up in London

1. B. He stole eggs from the hen house and threw them at the Jesuit priests.
2. A. Cocky
3. A. Hitchcock stood at the foot of his mother's bed while she interrogated him about his daily activities.
4. C. Hitchcock memorized the train timetables, and rode every tramline in London.
5. A. *Stage Fright*
6. D. He often visited the Old Bailey Court, watching murder trials.

QUIZ 65

Great Idea: Influences and Inspirations

1. Edgar Allen Poe
2. G. K. Chesterton
3. (William) Somerset Maugham
4. *Rear Window*
5. *The Wrong Man*
6. *The Man Who Knew Too Much* (1956)
7. During the filming of *The Birds*, a farmer living near Bodega Bay told Hitchcock about crows attacking the farmer's lambs.
8. Frank Lloyd Wright
9. *The Pleasure Garden*
10. *The Man Who Knew Too Much* (1934)

QUIZ 66

Hitchcock and His Blondes

1. D. Doris Day in *The Man Who Knew Too Much* (1956)
2. B. Anne Baxter in *I Confess* (1953)
3. G. Tippi Hedren
4. J. Janet Leigh in *Psycho* (1960)
5. C. Karen Black in *Family Plot* (1976)
6. L. Vera Miles
7. H. Grace Kelly in *To Catch a Thief* (1955)
8. A. Joan Barry, who supplied the voice of Anny Ondra in the sound version of *Blackmail* (1929), and later starred in *Rich and Strange* (1932)
9. K. Carole Lombard in *Mr. and Mrs. Smith* (1941)
10. F. Joan Fontaine in *Suspicion* (1941)
11. O. Ann Todd, star of *The Paradine Case* (1947), who also starred in David Lean's *The Passionate Friends/One Woman's Story* (1949), *Madeleine* (1950), and *Breaking Through the Sound Barrier* (1952)
12. E. Marlene Dietrich in *Stage Fright* (1950). She sings "I'm the Laziest Girl in Town."
13. M. Kim Novak in *Vertigo* (1958)
14. I. Priscilla Lane in *Saboteur* (1942), and the fight on the Statue of Liberty; or
15. N. Eva Marie Saint in *North by Northwest* (1959), with the fight on Mount Rushmore

chronology

1899 August 13: Alfred Joseph Hitchcock, the youngest of three children, is born to William and Emma Hitchcock in the East End of London, England. (Alfred's brother, William Jr., was born in 1890 and Alfred's sister, Ellen Kathleen, known as "Nellie," was born on September 14, 1892.)

1899 August 14: Alma Lucy Reville, Hitchcock's future wife, is born in Nottingham, England.

1910 October 5: Hitchcock is enrolled at the Saint Ignatius College in Stamford Hills, London.

1914 December 12: Hitchcock's father, William Hitchcock, grocer, dies from a perinephric abscess at age fifty-two.

1915 Winter: Hitchcock is employed as an estimator for Henley Telegraph and Cable Company in London.

1918 Hitchcock's short story, "Gas," appears in the first issue of *The Henley*, a magazine published by his employer.

1920 Spring: The Famous Players-Lasky film company in London hires Hitchcock as a part-time title designer for their silent films.

1921 Alma Reville, working as a film editor for Famous Players-Lasky, meets Alfred Hitchcock.

1923 Summer: Producer Michael Balcon hires Hitchcock as an assistant film director for Islington Studios in London.

1925 Spring: Michael Balcon offers Hitchcock the position of sole director of the silent movie, *The Pleasure Garden*. A film crew, which includes Alma Reville as assistant director, travels to Germany to produce the picture.

1926 December 2: Alma Reville and Alfred Hitchcock are married on a Thursday morning at a small chapel in the Roman Catholic parish of Knightsbridge, London.

1927 January 24: *The Pleasure Garden* is released and Hitchcock's first feature film is proclaimed a success by the London press.

July: Hitchcock makes his first cameo appearance in the silent film, *The Lodger*. He is standing with his back to the camera in a newspaper office.

September 30: Hitchcock's silent picture, *The Ring*, is screened for the press.

1928 July 7: Alfred and Alma Hitchcock's only child, Patricia, is born in the bedroom at their home on Cromwall Road in London, England.

1929 November: Hitchcock's debut sound feature film, *Blackmail*, is released by British International Pictures.

1931 Winter: The Hitchcocks begin their round-the-world vacation.

1933 Hitchcock directs his first and last costume-musical film, *Waltzes from Vienna*, released by the British company, Tom Arnold Productions.

1934 Spring: Hitchcock signs a five-film contract with Gaumont-British Pictures.

December: The first version of *The Man Who Knew Too Much* is released.

1937 August 22: Hitchcock and his family arrive in America for the first time. He claims that the trip is a family holiday, but it is well known that he is to meet with several Hollywood movie producers about directing films in the United States.

1938 July 2: David O. Selznick, head of Selznick International Pictures, announces to the press that an offer has been made to Hitchcock to direct a Hollywood film the following year.

July 14: Hitchcock signs a contract with Selznick International Pictures, but it is still unsure whether his first Hollywood production will be *The Titanic* or *Rebecca*.

October: Hitchcock makes his last movie for a British film company. The costume drama, *Jamaica Inn*, is released by Erich Pommer Productions in 1939.

1939 February: The Hitchcocks give up their apartment in London, sell their country home, Winter's Grace, in the village of Shamely Green, England, and move to California.

April 10: Hitchcock begins work for Selznick International Pictures in Los Angeles, California.

1940 March: Hitchcock's first American-made project, *Rebecca*, is released by Selznick Studios.

1941 November: *Suspicion*, a Selznick Studio film, starring Cary Grant and Joan Fontaine, is released by RKO.

1942 Patricia Hitchcock, now fourteen, debuts on Broadway in the play, *Solitaire*.

September 26: Emma Jane Whelan Hitchcock, Hitchcock's seventy-nine-year-old mother, dies in England on her fifty-fifth wedding anniversary from an abdominal fistula, and an acute intestinal abscess.

1943 January 4: Hitchcock's older brother William, age fifty-three, dies mysteriously at his home in England. It is believed that he committed suicide by taking paraldehyde, causing heart failure.

January: During the filming of *Lifeboat* (1944), a Twentieth Century-Fox release, Hitchcock goes on a serious diet, reducing his weight from 300 to 200 pounds.

1944 December 5: Hitchcock leaves for a fortnight in England to direct two short propaganda films, *Bon Voyage* and *Aventure Malgache*, showing his support for the World War II effort.

1946 April 11: A London periodical, *The Daily Film Renter*, reports that Hitchcock and producer Sydney Bernstein have formed a production company called Transatlantic Pictures.

1948 August: *Rope*, Hitchcock's first film as a producer for Transatlantic and one of four Hitchcock features starring James Stewart is released by Warner Bros. Pictures. This is also Hitchcock's first Technicolor movie.

1950 April 12: Hitchcock purchases the screen rights to Patricia Highsmith's novel *Strangers on a Train* for a mere $7,500. The 1951 release will feature Patricia Hitchcock in a supporting role.

1952 January: Patricia Hitchcock marries Joseph E. O'Connell, treasurer of the Thomas Dalby Corporation located in Watertown, Massachusetts.

1953 April 17: Mary O'Connell, the first of Hitchcock's three granddaughters is born, followed by Teresa, born on July 2, 1954, and Kathleen, born on February 27, 1959.

May: Hitchcock produces his first and only 3-D movie, *Dial M for Murder*, a Warner Bros. suspense drama, starring Ray Milland, Grace Kelly (first of three pictures for Hitchcock), and Robert Cummings. It is released in 1954.

Summer: Hitchcock signs a five-picture contract with Paramount Pictures, resulting in: *Rear Window* (1954), *The Trouble with Harry* (1955), *The Man Who Knew Too Much* (1956), *Vertigo* (1958), and *Psycho* (1960).

August: The world premiere of *Rear Window*, costarring James Stewart and Grace Kelly, is held at the Rivoli Theatre in New York.

1955 February: *Rear Window* earns Hitchcock a nomination for Best Director by the Academy of Motion Pictures Arts and Sciences. However, he loses to director Elia Kazan for *On the Waterfront* (1954).

April 20: Hitchcock becomes a U.S. citizen.

October 2: The premier episode of *Alfred Hitchcock Presents*, a half-hour anthology drama hosted by Hitchcock and filmed in black-and-white, debuts on CBS-TV.

1957 March 11: Hitchcock is hospitalized for what he suspects is a heart attack. Instead he undergoes gallbladder surgery, followed by a month-long recuperation at his home in Santa Rosa, California.

September: Filming begins on *Vertigo*, starring James Stewart and Kim Novak.

1958 April: Hitchcock wins the Golden Globe Award for Best Television Series of the year.

1959 August: *North by Northwest*, with Cary Grant and Eva Marie Saint, is released by Metro-Goldwyn-Mayer.

1959 September: *Alfred Hitchcock Presents* is moved to NBC-TV and expanded to sixty minutes under its new title, *The Alfred Hitchcock Hour*.

1960 February: Hitchcock gains another Oscar nomination as Best Director for the thriller *Psycho*, with Anthony Perkins and Janet Leigh. At the Oscars he loses to director Billy Wilder for *The Apartment*.

1961 Fall: While watching the *Today* show, Hitchcock notices an attractive blonde, Tippi Hedren, in a television commercial for the diet drink Sego. He makes an appointment to meet her the following day, and by the end of the week he offers her a seven-year film contract.

1963 March 29: *The Birds*, a Universal film, is released, followed by a publicity tour in the United States that includes Hitchcock, star Tippi Hedren, and several Universal executives.

September: Tippi Hedren and Sean Connery meet for the first time as filming for Hitchcock's *Marnie* (1964) begins at Universal.

1965 April: Hitchcock ends his decade-long television career.

1966 July: Hitchcock's fiftieth film, *Torn Curtain*, costarring Paul Newman and Julie Andrews, is released by Universal.

1968 April 10: The Academy of Motion Picture Arts and Sciences presents Hitchcock with a special Oscar, the Irving G. Thalberg Memorial Award.

May 3: Hitchcock and author Leon Uris announce to the media at the Saint Regis Hotel in New York that filming of Uris' novel *Topaz* (Universal) is scheduled for October.

1971 Summer: Hitchcock gathers his movie crew and returns to London to shoot what is to become his best feature film in a decade, the thriller *Frenzy*.

1972 May 25: The world premiere of *Frenzy*, a Universal picture, takes place in London, England.

1976 April: Hitchcock's last film, *Family Plot*, a macabre comedy, is released by Universal on the first night of the Los Angeles Film Festival.

December 2: Alfred and Alma Hitchcock celebrate their fiftieth wedding anniversary.

1979 March 12: The American Film Institute honors Hitchcock with its seventh Life Achievement Award.

1980 January 3: Hitchcock is made a Knight Commander of the British Empire by Queen Elizabeth II. Thomas W. Aston, the British consul general, administers the knighthood in Hitchcock's office at Universal Studios.

March 16: Hitchcock makes his last public appearance at the American Film Institute's annual awards ceremony, where it is customary for a previous year's recipient to introduce the new winner.

April 29: At 9:17 A.M., Alfred Hitchcock, age eighty, dies at his home in Los Angeles of liver failure and other complications.

1988 April 20: American Playhouse airs the remake of the 1941 movie *Suspicion*. The PBS-TV production stars Jane Curtin as Lina McLaidlaw, and British actor Anthony Andrews as Johnny Aysgarth.

1996 April 19: *Entertainment Weekly* ranks Hitchcock number one on its list of the fifty greatest film directors of all time.

April: The restored *Vertigo* (1958) is re-released in seventy-millimeter format.

November 21: The British version of *Strangers on a Train* (1951), two minutes longer than the original American print, is released for home video.

1997 September: Universal Pictures announces that it has begun restoring *Rear Window* (1954) and expects to complete the task in about eighteen months.

October: The U.S. Postal Service issues an Alfred Hitchcock 32¢ commemorative stamp.

1998 June 5: *A Perfect Murder*, directed by Andrew Davis and based on Frederick Knott's play *Dial M for Murder*, stars Michael Douglas and Gwyneth Paltrow. It is released by Warner Bros. (Hitchcock's version of *Dial M for Murder* had appeared in 1954).

November 22: The retelling of Alfred Hitchcock's *Rear Window* (1954) airs on ABC television. Christopher Reeve, in his first acting performance since his debilitating horseback-riding accident, proves to have made a heroic effort as an actor as well as a man struggling with his own disabilities. *Hollywood Reporter* critic Irv Letofsky credits Reeve with doing an "excellent, sometimes wrenching job." However, the reviewer adds that the newer version of *Rear Window*—directed by Jeff Bleckner and costarring Daryl Hannah and Robert Forster—does not live up to the fine reputation of the original 1950s version.

December 4: The remake of Alfred Hitchcock's classic thriller *Psycho* (1960) is released. Following in Hitchcock's footsteps, producer Brian Grazer does not allow for sneak previews or a press screening before the actual release. Kenneth Turan (*Los Angeles Times*) refers to director Gus Van Sant's scene-by-scene remake (which is shot in color in contrast to the original's black-and-white cinematography) as a gimmick and a waste of time and money. In its first thirty-eight days of domestic release, the "new" *Psycho*, starring Vince Vaughn (as Norman Bates), Anne Heche (as Marion Crane), and Julianne Moore (as Lila Crane), grosses a very disappointing $21,133,025.

1999 Toward the end of the year: The recently restored *Rear Window* (1954) will be released.

Filmography

FEATURE-LENGTH FILMS DIRECTED BY ALFRED HITCHCOCK

Silent Features

The Pleasure Garden (GAINSBOROUGH/EMELKA , 1925), B&W, 85 MINUTES.

Producer: Michael Balcon; *Screenplay*: Eliot Stannard (based on the novel by Oliver Sandys); *Director of Photography*: Baron [Giovanni] Ventimiglia.

Cast: Virginia Valli (Patsy Brand); Carmelita Geraghty (Jill Cheyne); Miles Mander (Levett); John Stuart (Hugh Fielding); Nita Naldi (Native girl); and: Frederick Martini, Florence Helminger.

The Mountain Eagle (GAINSBOROUGH/EMELKA, 1925), B&W, 85 MINUTES.

Producer: Michael Balcon; *Screenplay*: Eliot Stannard; *Director of Photography*: Baron [Giovanni] Ventimiglia.

Cast: Bernhard Goetzke (Mr. Pettigrew); Nita Naldi (Beatrice); Malcolm Keen (Fear o' God Fulton); John Hamilton (Edward Pettigrew).

(U.S. release title: *Fear o' God*)

The Lodger: A Story of the London Fog (GAINSBOROUGH, 1926), B&W, 125 MINUTES.

Producer: Michael Balcon; *Screenplay*: Eliot Stannard (based on the novel by Marie Belloc); *Director of Photography*: Baron [Giovanni] Ventimiglia; *Assistant Director*: Alma Reville; *Art Directors/Production Designers*: C. Wilfrid Arnold and Bertram Evans; *Editor/Titling*: Ivor Montagu; *Title Designs*: E. McKnight Kauffer.

Cast: Marie Ault (The landlady); Arthur Chesney (Her husband); June (Daisy Bunting, a mannequin); Malcolm Keen (Joe, a police detective); Ivor Novello (The lodger).

(U.S. release title: *The Case of Jonathan Drew*)

Downhill (GAINSBOROUGH, 1927), B&W, 95 MINUTES.

Producer: Michael Balcon; *Screenplay*: Eliot Stannard (based on the play by David LeStrange, pseudonym of Ivor Novello and Constance Collier); *Director of Photography*: Claude McDonnell; *Editor*: Ivor Montagu.

Cast: Ivor Novello (Roddy Berwick); Robin Irvine (Tim Wakely); Lillian Braithwaite (Lady Berwick); Isabel Jeans (Julia); Ian Hunter (Archie).

(U.S. release title: *When Boys Leave Home*)

Easy Virtue (GAINSBOROUGH, 1927), B&W, 75 MINUTES.

Producer: Michael Balcon; *Screenplay*: Eliot Stannard (based on the play by Noel Coward); *Director of Photography*: Claude McDonnell; *Editor*: Ivor Montagu.

Cast: Isabel Jeans (Larita Filton); Franklyn Dyall (Her husband); Eric Bransby Williams (The artist); Ian Hunter (Counsel for the plaintiff); Robin Irvine (John Whittaker); Violet Farebrother (His mother); and: Benita Hume.

The Ring (BRITISH INTERNATIONAL, 1927), B&W, 30 MINUTES.

Producer: John Maxwell; *Screenplay*: Alfred Hitchcock; *Director of Photography*: John J. Cox; *Continuity Supervisor*: Alma Reville.

Cast: Carl Brisson (Jack Sanders); Lillian Hall Davis (Nellie); Ian Hunter (The champion); and: Harry Terry, Gordon Harker, Forrester Harvey, Tom Helmore.

The Farmer's Wife (BRITISH INTERNATIONAL, 1928), B&W, 156 MINUTES.

Producer: John Maxwell; *Screenplay*: Alfred Hitchcock (based on the play by Eden Phillpotts); *Director of Photography*: John J. Cox; *Editor*: Alfred Booth.

Cast: Jameson Thomas (Farmer Sweetland); Lillian Hall Davis (Araminta Dench); Gordon Harker (Churdles Ash); Maud Gill (Thirza Tapper); Louise Pounds (Widow Windeat); and: Olga Slade, Antonia Brough.

Champagne (BRITISH INTERNATIONAL, 1928), B&W, 75 MINUTES.

Producer: John Maxwell; *Screenplay*: Eliot Stannard (based on an original story by Walter C. Mycroft); *Adaptation*: Alfred Hitchcock; *Director of Photography*: John J. Cox; *Assistant Director*: Frank Mills; *Art Director/Production Designer*: C. W. Arnold.

Cast: Betty Balfour (The girl); Jean Bradin (The boy); Theo von Alten (The man); Gordon Harker (The father).

The Manxman (BRITISH INTERNATIONAL, 1929), B&W, 129 MINUTES.

Producer: John Maxwell; *Screenplay*: Eliot Stannard (based on the novel by Hall Caine); *Director of Photography*: John J. Cox; *Assistant Director*: Frank Mills.

Cast: Carl Brisson (Pete); Malcolm Keen (Philip); Anny Ondra (Kate); Randle Ayrton (Her father).

Sound Features

Blackmail (BRITISH INTERNATIONAL, 1929), B&W, 86 MINUTES.

Producer: John Maxwell; *Screenplay*: Alfred Hitchcock (based on the play by Charles Bennett); *Dialogue*: Benn W. Levy; *Director of Photography*: John J. Cox; *Assistant Director*: Frank Mills; *Art Director/Production Designer*: C. W. Arnold; *Music*: Campbell and Connelly; *Editor*: Emile de Ruelle.

Cast: Anny Ondra (Alice White) [voice: Joan Barry]; Sara Allgood (Mrs. White); Charles Paton (Mr. White); John Longden (Detective Frank Webber); Donald Calthrop (Tracy, the blackmailer); Cyril Ritchard (The artist); Hannah Jones (The landlady); Phyllis Monkman (The neighbor); Harvey Braban (Chief inspector).

Juno and the Paycock (BRITISH INTERNATIONAL, 1930), B&W, 95 MINUTES.

Producer: John Maxwell; *Adaptation*: Alfred Hitchcock and Alma Reville (based on the play by Sean O'Casey); *Director of Photography*: John J. Cox; *Art Director/Production Designer*: Norman Arnold.

Cast: Sara Allgood (Juno); Edward Chapman (Captain Boyle); Marie O'Neill (Mrs. Madigan); Sidney Morgan (Joxer); Kathleen O'Regan (Mary Boyle).

(U.S. release title: *The Shame of Mary Boyle*)

Murder! (BRITISH INTERNATIONAL, 1930), B&W, 100 MINUTES.

Producer: John Maxwell; *Screenplay*: Alma Reville; *Adaptation*: Alfred Hitchcock and Walter Mycroft (based on the novel and play *Enter Sir John* by Clemence Dane and Helen Simpson); *Director of Photography*: John J. Cox; *Assistant Director*: Frank Mills; *Art Director/Production Designer*: J. F. Mead; *Music*: John Reynders; *Editors*: René Harrison and Emile de Ruelle.

Cast: Norah Baring (Diana Baring); Herbert Marshall (Sir John Menier); Miles Mander (Gordon Druce); Esmé Percy (Handel Fane); and: Edward Chapman, Phyllis Konstam, Hannah Jones, Una O'Connor .

(German-language version, directed by Hitchcock and starring Walter Abel, was titled *Mary*)

The Skin Game (BRITISH INTERNATIONAL, 1931), B&W, 86 MINUTES.

Producer: John Maxwell; *Screenplay*: Alma Reville (based on the play by John Galsworthy); *Adaptation*: Alfred Hitchcock; *Director of Photography*: John J. Cox; *Assistant Director*: Frank Mills; *Art Director/Production Designer*: J. B. Maxwell.

Cast: C. V. France (Mr. Hillcrist); Helen Hayes (Mrs. Hillcrist); Edmund Gwenn (Mr. Hornblower); Jill Esmond (Jill); John Longden (Charles Hornblower); Phyllis Konstam (Chloe Hornblower).

Rich and Strange (BRITISH INTERNATIONAL, 1932). B&W, 83 MINUTES.

Producer: John Maxwell; *Screenplay*: Alma Reville; *Adaptation*: Alfred Hitchcock; *Additional Dialogue*: Val Valentine; *Directors of Photography*: John J. Cox and Charles Martin; *Assistant Director*: Frank Mills; *Art Director/Production Designer*: C. W. Arnold; *Music*: Hal Dolphe; *Editors*: René Harrison and Winifred Cooper.

Cast: Henry Kendall (Fred Hill); Joan Barry (Emily Hill); Percy Marmont (Commander Gordon); Betty Amann (The "Princess"); Elsie Randolph (The old maid).

(U.S. release title: *East of Shanghai*)

Number Seventeen (BRITISH INTERNATIONAL, 1932), B&W, 61 MINUTES.

Producer: John Maxwell; *Screenplay*: Alma Reville, Alfred Hitchcock, and Rodney Ackland (based on the play by J. Jefferson Farjeon); *Directors of Photography*: John J. Cox and Bryan Langley; *Assistant Director*: Frank Mills; *Art Director/ Production Designer*: C. W. Arnold; *Music*: A. Hallis; *Editor*: A. C. Hammond.

Cast: Leon M. Lion (Ben); Anne Grey (The girl); John Stuart (The detective); and: Donald Calthrop, Barry Jones, Ann Casson, Henry Caine, Garry Marsh.

Waltzes from Vienna (GAUMONT-BRITISH, 1933), B&W, 95 MINUTES.

Producer: Tom Arnold; *Screenplay*: Alma Reville and Guy Bolton (based on the play by Guy Bolton); *Art Director/Production Designer*: Alfred Junge; *Set Designer*: Peter Proud; *Music*: Johann Strauss Jr.

Cast: Jessie Matthews (Rasi); Esmond Knight (Johann Strauss Jr); Edmund Gwenn (Johann Strauss Sr); Frank Vosper (The prince); Fay Compton (The countess).

(U.S. release title: *Strauss's Great Waltz*)

The Man Who Knew Too Much (GAUMONT-BRITISH, 1934), B&W, 110 MINUTES.

Producer: Michael Balcon; *Associate Producer*: Ivor Montagu; *Screenplay*: Edwin Greenwood and A. R. Rawlinson (based on a story by Charles Bennett and D. B. Wyndham Lewis); *Additional Dialogue*: Emilyn Williams; *Director of Photography*: Curt Courant; *Art Director/Production Designer*: Alfred Junge; *Music*: Arthur Benjamin; *Editor*: H. St. C. Stewart.

Cast: Leslie Banks (Bob Lawrence); Edna Best (Jill Lawrence); Nova Pilbeam (Betty Lawrence); Peter Lorre (Abbott); Frank Vosper (Ramon); Hugh Wakefield (Clive); Pierre Fresnay (Louis Bernard); Cicely Oates (Nurse Agnes); and: D. A. Clarke-Smith, George Curzon.

The 39 Steps (GAUMONT-BRITISH, 1935), B&W, 81 MINUTES.

Producer: Michael Balcon; *Associate Producer*: Ivor Montagu; *Adaptation*: Charles Bennett (based on the novel by John Buchan); *Dialogue*: Ian Hay; *Continuity Supervisor*: Alma Reville; *Director of Photography*: Bernard Knowles; *Art Director/Production Designer*: O. Werndorff; *Music*: Louis Levy; *Editor*: D. N. Twist.

Cast: Robert Donat (Richard Hannay); Madeleine Carroll (Pamela); Lucie Mannheim (Annabella Smith); Godfrey Tearle (Professor Jordan); John Laurie (The crofter); Peggy Ashcroft (His wife); Helen Haye (Mrs. Jordan); Frank Cellier (The sheriff); Wylie Watson (Mr. Memory); and: Gus MacNaughton, Jerry Verno, Peggy Simpson.

Secret Agent (GAUMONT-BRITISH, 1936), B&W, 95 MINUTES.

Producer: Michael Balcon; *Associate Producer*: Ivor Montagu; *Screenplay*: Charles Bennett (from the play by Campbell Dixon, based on stories by W. Somerset

Maugham); *Dialogue*: Ian Hay and Jesse Lasky Jr.; *Continuity Supervisor*: Alma Reville; *Director of Photography*: Bernard Knowles; *Art Director/Production Designer*: O. Werndorff; *Music*: Louis Levy; *Editor*: Charles Frend.

Cast: John Gielgud (Edgar Brodie/Richard Ashenden); Madeleine Carroll (Elsa Carrington); Peter Lorre (The general); Robert Young (Robert Marvin); Percy Marmont (Caypor); Florence Kahn (Mrs. Caypor); and: Charles Carson, Lilli Palmer, Michel Saint-Denis.

Sabotage (GAUMONT-BRITISH, 1936), B&W, 77 MINUTES.

Producer: Michael Balcon; *Associate Producer*: Ivor Montagu; *Screenplay*: Charles Bennett (based on the novel *The Secret Agent* by Joseph Conrad); *Dialogue*: Ian Hay and Helen Simpson; *Continuity Supervisor*: Alma Reville; *Director of Photography*: Bernard Knowles; *Art Director/Production Designer*: O. Werndorff; *Music*: Louis Levy; *Editor*: Charles Frend.

Cast: Sylvia Sidney (Mrs. Verloc); Oscar Homolka (Mr. Verloc); Desmond Tester (Stevie); John Loder (Ted Spenser); Joyce Barbour (Renee); and: William Dewhurst, Martita Hunt, Peter Bull.

(U.S. release title: *The Woman Alone*)

Young and Innocent (GAUMONT-BRITISH, 1937), B&W, 84 MINUTES.

Producer: Edward Black; *Screenplay*: Charles Bennett, Edwin Greenwood, and Anthony Armstrong (based on the novel *A Shilling for Candles* by Josephine Tey); *Dialogue*: Gerald Savory; *Continuity Supervisor*: Alma Reville; *Director of Photography*: Bernard Knowles; *Art Director/Production Designer*: Alfred Junge; *Music*: Louis Levy; *Editor*: Charles Frend.

Cast: Nova Pilbeam (Erica Burgoyne); Derrick de Marney (Robert Tisdall); Percy Marmont (Colonel Burgoyne); Edward Rigby (Old Will); Mary Clare (Erica's aunt); John Longden (Detective Inspector Kent); George Curzon (Guy); Basil Radford (Erica's Uncle); Pamela Carme (Christine Clay).

(U.S. release title: *The Girl Was Young*)

The Lady Vanishes (GAUMONT-BRITISH, 1938), B&W, 96 MINUTES.

Producer: Edward Black; *Screenplay*: Sidney Gilliat and Frank Launder (based on the novel *The Wheel Spins* by Ethel Lina White); *Continuity Supervisor*: Alma Reville; *Director of Photography*: John J. Cox; *Set Designer*: Vetchinsky; *Music*: Louis Levy; *Editor*: R. E. Dearing.

Cast: Margaret Lockwood (Iris Henderson); Michael Redgrave (Gilbert); Dame May Whitty (Miss Froy); Paul Lukas (Dr. Hartz); Cecil Parker (Mr. Todhunter); Linden Travers (His mistress); Naunton Wayne (Caldicott); Basil Radford (Charters); Mary Clare (Baroness); Catherine Lacey (The "nun"); and: Josephine Wilson, Kathleen Tremaine, Emile Boreo, Googie Withers.

Jamaica Inn (ERICH POMMER/MAYFLOWER, 1939), B&W, 99 MINUTES.

Producer: Erich Pommer; *Screenplay*: Sidney Gilliat and Joan Harrison (based on the novel by Daphne du Maurier); *Additional Dialogue*: J. B. Priestley; *Continuity Supervisor*: Alma Reville; *Director of Photography*: Harry Stradling and Bernard Knowles; *Set Designer*: Tom Morahan; *Wardrobe and Costumes*: Molly McArthur; *Music*: Eric Fenby; *Editor*: Robert Hamer.

Cast: Charles Laughton (Sir Humphrey Pengallan); Leslie Banks (Joss Merlyn); Marie Ney (Patience, his wife); Maureen O'Hara (Mary, his niece); Emlyn Williams (Harry); Wylie Watson (Salvation); Mervyn Johns (Thomas); Robert Newton (Jem Traherne); and: Edwin Greenwood, Stephen Haggard.

Rebecca (SELZNICK STUDIO/RKO, 1940), B&W, 130 MINUTES.

Producer: David O. Selznick; *Screenplay*: Robert E. Sherwood and Joan Harrison (based on the novel by Daphne du Maurier); *Adaptation*: Philip MacDonald and Michael Hogan; *Director of Photography*: George Barnes; *Assistant Director*: Edmond Bernoudy; *Art Director/Production Designer*: Lyle Wheeler; *Set Designer*: Joseph B. Platt; *Special Effects Supervisor*: Jack Cosgrove; *Music*: Franz Waxman; *Editors*: James Newcom and Hal Kern.

Cast: Laurence Olivier (Maxim de Winter); Joan Fontaine (His wife), Judith Anderson (Mrs. Danvers); George Sanders (Jack Favell); Florence Bates (Mrs. Van Hopper); Nigel Bruce (Giles Lacey); Gladys Cooper (Beatrice Lacey); and: C. Aubrey Smith, Melville Cooper, Leo G. Carroll, Forrester Harvey, Reginald Denny, Lumsden Hare, Philip Winter, Edward Fielding.

Foreign Correspondent (WANGER PRODUCTIONS/UNITED ARTISTS, 1940), B&W, 120 MINUTES.

Producer: Walter Wanger; *Screenplay*: Charles Bennett and Joan Harrison; *Dialogue*: James Hilton and Robert Benchley; *Director of Photography*: Rudolph Maté; *Assistant Director*: Edmond Bernoudy; *Art Director/Production Designer*: Alexander Golitzen; *Set Designer*: Julia Heron; *Special Effects Supervisor*: Paul Eagler; *Special Production Effects*: William Cameron Menzies; *Wardrobe and*

Costumes: I. Magnin; *Music*: Alfred Newman; *Editors*: Otho Lovering and Dorothy Spencer.

Cast: Joel McCrea (Johnny Jones/Huntley Haverstock); Laraine Day (Carol Fisher); Herbert Marshall (Stephen Fisher); George Sanders (ffolliott); Albert Basserman (Van Meer); Robert Benchley (Stebbins); Edmund Gwenn (Rowley); Harry Davenport (Mr. Powers); Eduardo Ciannelli (Krug); and: Eddie Conrad, Frances Carson, Martin Kosleck, Gertrude W. Hoffman, Emory Parnell, Ian Wolfe, Eily Malyon, E. E. Clive.

Mr. and Mrs. Smith (RKO, 1941), B&W, 93 MINUTES.

Producer: Harry E. Edington; *Story and Screenplay*: Norman Krasna; *Director of Photography*: Harry Stradling; *Assistant Director*: Dewey Starkey; *Art Director/ Production Designer*: Van Nest Polglase; *Set Designer*: Darrell Silvera; *Special Effects Supervisor*: Vernon L. Walker; *Wardrobe and Costumes*: Irene; *Music*: Edward Wand; *Editor*: William Hamilton.

Cast: Carole Lombard (Ann Krausheimer Smith); Robert Montgomery (David Smith); Gene Raymond (Jeff Custer); Philip Merivale (His father); Lucile Watson (His mother); Jack Carson (Chuck Benson).

Suspicion (RKO, 1941), B&W, 99 MINUTES.

Producer: Harry E. Eddington; *Screenplay*: Samson Raphaelson, Joan Harrison, and Alma Reville (based on the novel *Before the Fact* by Francis Iles); *Director of Photography*: Harry Stradling; *Assistant Director*: Dewey Starkey; *Art Director/ Production Designer*: Van Nest Polglase; *Set Designer*: Darrell Silvera; *Special Effects Supervisor*: Vernon L. Walker; *Music*: Franz Waxman; *Editor*: William Hamilton.

Cast: Joan Fontaine (Lina McLaidlaw); Cary Grant (Johnny Aysgarth); Sir Cedric Hardwicke (General McLaidlaw); Dame May Whitty (Mrs. McLaidlaw); Nigel Bruce (Beaky Thwaite); Isabel Jeans (Mrs. Newsham); and: Heather Angel, Auriol Lee, Leo G. Carroll.

Saboteur (UNIVERSAL, 1942), B&W, 77 MINUTES.

Producer: Frank Lloyd; *Associate Producer*: Jack H. Skirball; *Screenplay*: Peter Viertel, Joan Harrison, and Dorothy Parker; *Director of Photography*: Joseph Valentine; *Assistant Director*: Fred Rank; *Art Directors/Production Designers*: Jack Otterson and Robert Boyle; *Music*: Frank Skinner; *Editor*: Otto Ludwig.

Cast: Robert Cummings (Barry Kane); Priscilla Lane (Pat Martin); Otto Kruger (Charles Tobin); Alma Kruger (Mrs. Van Sutton); Norman Lloyd (Fry).

Shadow of a Doubt (UNIVERSAL, 1943), B&W, 108 MINUTES.

Producer: Jack H. Skirball; *Screenplay*: Thornton Wilder, Sally Benson, and Alma Reville (based on an original story by Gordon McDonell); *Director of Photography*: Joseph Valentine; *Assistant Director*: William Tummell; *Art Directors/ Production Designers*: John B. Goodman and Robert Boyle; *Set Designers*: R. A. Gausman and E. R. Robinson; *Wardrobe and Costumes*: Adrian and Vera West; *Music*: Dimitri Tiomkin; *Editor*: Milton Carruth.

Cast: Joseph Cotten (Uncle Charlie Oakley); Teresa Wright (Charlie Newton); Macdonald Carey (Jack Graham); Patricia Collinge (Emma Newton); Henry Travers (Joe Newton); Hume Cronyn (Herb Hawkins); Edna May Wonacott (Ann Newton); Charles Bates (Roger Newton); Wallace Ford (Fred Saunders); and: Eily Malyon, Estelle Jewell.

Lifeboat (TWENTIETH CENTURY-FOX, 1944), B&W, 96 MINUTES.

Producer: Kenneth MacGowan; *Screenplay*: Jo Swerling (based on a story by John Steinbeck); *Director of Photography*: Glen MacWilliams; *Art Directors/Production Supervisors*: James Basevi and Maurice Ransford; *Set Designers*: Thomas Little and Frank E. Hughes; *Special Effects Supervisor*: Fred Sersen; *Technical Advisor*: Thomas Fitzsimmons; *Wardrobe and Costumes*: René Hubert; *Music*: Hugo W. Friedhofer; *Editor*: Dorothy Spencer.

Cast: Tallulah Bankhead (Constance [Connie] Porter); John Hodiak (Kovak); William Bendix (Gus); Walter Slezak (Willi); Mary Anderson (Alice MacKenzie); Hume Cronyn (Stanley Garrett); Henry Hull (Charles J. Rittenhouse); Heather Angel (Mrs. Higgins); Canada Lee (Joe Spencer).

Spellbound (SELZNICK INTERNATIONAL/UNITED ARTISTS, 1945), B&W, 111 MINUTES.

Producer: David O. Selznick; *Screenplay*: Ben Hecht (based on the novel *The House of Dr. Edwardes* by Francis Beeding); *Adaptation*: Angus MacPhail; *Director of Photography*: George Barnes; *Assistant Director*: Lowell J. Farrell; *Art Director/ Production Designer*: James Basevi; *Set Designer*: Emile Kuri; *Special Effects Supervisor*: Jack Cosgrove; *Dream Sequence* based on designs by Salvador Dali; *Medical Advisor*: Dr. May E. Romm; *Music*: Miklos Rozsa; *Editor*: Hal Kern.

Cast: Ingrid Bergman (Dr. Constance Petersen); Gregory Peck (John Ballantine); Leo G. Carroll (Dr. Murchison); Norman Lloyd (Garmes); Rhonda Fleming (Mary Carmichael); Michael Chekhov (Dr. Alex Brulov), John Emery (Dr. Fleurot); Edward Fielding (Dr. Edwards); and: Bill Goodwin, Art Baker, Wallace Ford.

Notorious (RKO, 1946), B&W, 101 MINUTES.

Producer: Alfred Hitchcock; *Screenplay*: Ben Hecht; *Director of Photography*: Ted Tetzlaff; *Assistant Director*: William Dorfman; *Art Directors/Production Designers*: Albert S. D'Agostino and Carroll Clark; *Set Designers*: Darrell Silvera and Claude Carpenter; *Special Effects Supervisors*: Vernon L. Walker and Paul Eagler; *Wardrobe and Costumes*: Edith Head; *Music*: Roy Webb; *Editor*: Theron Warth.

Cast: Ingrid Bergman (Alicia Huberman); Cary Grant (T. R. Devlin); Claude Rains (Alexander Sebastian); Leopoldine Konstantin (Madame Sebastian); Louis Calhern (Paul Prescott); Reinhold Schunzel (Dr. Anderson); Ivan Triesault (Eric Mathis); Alex Minotis (Joseph); Eberhard Krumschmidt (Hupka); Sir Charles Mendl (Commodore); Moroni Olsen (Walter Beardsley); Ricardo Costa (Dr. Barbosa).

The Paradine Case (SELZNICK/VANGUARD/UNITED ARTISTS, 1947), B&W, 85 MINUTES.

Producer: David O. Selznick; *Screenplay*: David O. Selznick (based on the novel by Robert Hichens); *Adaptation*: Alma Reville; *Director of Photography*: Lee Garmes; *Assistant Director*: Lowell J. Farrell; *Art Director*: Tom Morahan; *Production Designer*: J. MacMillan Johnson; *Set Designers*: Joseph B. Platt and Emile Kuri; *Special Effects Supervisor*: Clarence Silfer; *Wardrobe and Costumes*: Travis Banton; *Music*: Franz Waxman; *Editors*: Hal Kern and John Faure.

Cast: Gregory Peck (Anthony Keane); (Alida)Valli (Maddalena Paradine); Ann Todd (Gay, his wife); Charles Laughton (Lord Horfield); Ethel Barrymore (Lady Horfield); Charles Coburn (Sir Simon Flaquer); Joan Tetzel (Judy Flaquer, his daughter); Louis Jourdan (André Latour); and: Leo G. Carroll, John Williams, Isobel Elsom.

Rope (TRANSATLANTIC/WARNER BROS., 1948), COLOR, 81 MINUTES.

Producers: Alfred Hitchcock and Sidney Bernstein; *Screenplay*: Arthur Laurents (based on the play by Patrick Hamilton); *Adaptation*: Hume Cronyn; *Directors of Photography*: Joseph Valentine and William V. Skall; *Assistant Director*: Lowell J. Farrell; *Art Director/Production Designer*: Perry Ferguson; *Set Designers*: Emile Kuri and Howard Bristol; *Music*: Francis Poulenc and Leo F. Forbstein; *Editor*: William H. Ziegler.

Cast: James Stewart (Rupert Cadell); John Dall (Brandon); Farley Granger (Philip); Sir Cedric Hardwicke (Mr. Kentley); Constance Collier (Mrs. Atwater); Douglas Dick (Kenneth); Edith Evanson (Mrs. Wilson); Joan Chandler (Janet); Dick Hogan (David Kentley).

Under Capricorn (TRANSATLANTIC/WARNER BROS., 1949), COLOR,
117 MINUTES.

Producers: Alfred Hitchcock and Sidney Bernstein; *Screenplay*: James Bridie (from the
play by John Colton and Margaret Linden, based on the novel by Helen
Simpson); *Adaptation*: Hume Cronyn; *Continuity Supervisor*: Peggy Singer;
Director of Photography: Jack Cardiff; *Assistant Director*: C. Foster Kemp; *Art
Director/Production Designer*: Tom Morahan; *Wardrobe and Costumes*: Roger
Furse; *Music*: Richard Addinsell; *Editor*: A. S. Bates.

Cast: Joseph Cotten (Sam Flusky); Ingrid Bergman (Lady Henrietta Flusky); Michael
Wilding (Charles Adare); Margaret Leighton (Milly); Cecil Parker (Governor);
Denis O'Dea (Corrigan).

Stage Fright (WARNER BROS., 1950), B&W, 110 MINUTES.

Producer: Alfred Hitchcock; *Screenplay*: Whitfield Cook (based on the novel *Man
Running* by Selwyn Jepson); *Adaptation*: Alma Reville; *Continuity Supervisor*:
Peggy Singer; *Director of Photography*: Wilkie Cooper; *Art Director/Production
Designer*: Terence Verity; *Music*: Leighton Lucas; *Editor*: E. B. Jarvis.

Cast: Marlene Dietrich (Charlotte Inwood); Jane Wyman (Eve Gill); Michael Wilding
(Wilfrid Smith); Richard Todd (Jonathan "Johnny" Cooper); Alastair Sim
(Commodore Gill); Sybil Thorndike (Mrs. Gill); Kay Walsh (Nellie Good);
Patricia Hitchcock (Chubby Bannister); and: Joyce Grenfell, Miles Malleson,
Hector MacGregor, Ballard Berkeley, Andre Morell.

Strangers on a Train (WARNER BROS., 1951), B&W, 103 MINUTES.

Producer: Alfred Hitchcock; *Screenplay*: Raymond Chandler and Czenzi Ormonde
(based on the novel by Patricia Highsmith); *Adaptation*: Whitfield Cook; *Director
of Photography*: Robert Burks; *Art Director/Production Designer*: Edward S.
Haworth; *Set Designer*: George James Hopkins; *Special Effects Supervisor*: H. F.
Koenekamp; *Music*: Dimitri Tiomkin; *Editor*: William H. Ziegler.

Cast: Robert Walker (Bruno Anthony); Farley Granger (Guy Haines); Laura Elliott
(Miriam Haines); Ruth Roman (Ann Morton); Patricia Hitchcock (Barbara
Morton); Leo G. Carroll (Senator Morton); Marion Lorne (Mrs. Anthony); and:
Jonathan Hale, Norma Varden.

I Confess (WARNER BROS., 1953), B&W, 95 MINUTES.

Producer: Alfred Hitchcock; *Screenplay*: George Tabori and William Archibald (based
on the play *Nos Deux Consciences* by Paul Anthelme); *Director of Photography*:
Robert Burks; *Assistant Director*: Don Page; *Art Director/Production Designer*:

Edward S. Haworth; *Set Designer*: George James Hopkins; *Music*: Dimitri Tiomkin; *Editor*: Rudi Fehr.

Cast: Montgomery Clift (Father Michael Logan); Anne Baxter (Ruth Grandfort); Karl Malden (Inspector Larrue); Roger Dann (Pierre Grandfort); O. E. Hasse (Otto Keller); Dolly Haas (Alma Keller); Brian Aherne (Willy Robertson).

Dial M for Murder (WARNER BROS., 1954), COLOR, 105 MINUTES.

Producer: Alfred Hitchcock; *Screenplay*: Frederick Knott (based on his play); *Director of Photography*: Robert Burks; *Assistant Director*: Mel Dellar; *Art Director/Production Designer*: Edward Carrera; *Set Designer*: George James Hopkins; *Music*: Dimitri Tiomkin; *Editor*: Rudi Fehr.

Cast: Ray Milland (Tony Wendice); Grace Kelly (Margot Wendice); Robert Cummings (Mark Halliday); Anthony Dawson (Lesgate [Swan]); John Williams (Inspector Hubbard); Ovila Legare (Villette the lawyer); and: Leo Britt, Patrick Allen, George Leigh, George Alderson, Robin Hughes.

Rear Window (PARAMOUNT, 1954), COLOR, 113 MINUTES.

Producer: Alfred Hitchcock; *Screenplay*: John Michael Hayes (based on the short story by Cornell Woolrich); *Director of Photography*: Robert Burks; *Assistant Director*: Herbert Coleman; *Art Directors/Production Designers*: Hal Pereira and Joseph MacMillan Johnson; *Set Designers*: Sam Comer and Ray Moyer; *Special Effects Supervisor*: John P. Fulton; *Wardrobe and Costumes*: Edith Head; *Music*: Franz Waxman; *Editor*: George Tomasini.

Cast: James Stewart (L. B. Jeffries); Grace Kelly (Lisa Carol Fremont); Wendell Corey (Tom Doyle); Thelma Ritter (Stella); Raymond Burr (Lars Thorwald); Judith Evelyn (Miss Lonelyhearts); Irene Winston (Mrs. Thorwald); Ross Bagdasarian (The composer); Georgine Darcy (Miss Torso); Jesslyn Fax (Miss Sculptress); and: Sara Berner, Frank Cady, Rand Harper, Havis Davenport, Anthony Ward.

To Catch a Thief (PARAMOUNT, 1955), COLOR, 103 MINUTES.

Producer: Alfred Hitchcock; *Screenplay*: John Michael Hayes (based on the novel by David Dodge); *Director of Photography*: Robert Burks; *Second-Unit Director*: Herbert Coleman; *Second-Unit Director of Photography*: Wallace Kelley; *Process Photography*: Farciot Edouart; *Assistant Director*: Daniel McCauley; *Art Directors/Production Designers*: Hal Pereira and Joseph MacMillan Johnson; *Set Designers*: Sam Comer and Arthur Krams; *Special Effects Supervisor*: John P. Fulton; *Wardrobe and Costumes*: Edith Head; *Music*: Lyn Murray; *Editor*: George Tomasini.

Cast: Grace Kelly (Frances Stevens); Cary Grant (John Robie); Jessie Royce Landis (Jessie Stevens); John Williams (H. H. Hughson); Brigitte Auber (Danielle Foussard); Charles Vanel (Bertani); and: Rene Blancard.

The Trouble with Harry (PARAMOUNT, 1955), COLOR, 100 MINUTES.

Producer: Alfred Hitchcock; *Screenplay*: John Michael Hayes (based on the novel by J. Trevor Story); *Director of Photography*: Robert Burks; *Assistant Director*: Howard Joslin; *Art Director/Production Designer*: Herbert Coleman; *Wardrobe and Costumes*: Edith Head; *Music*: Bernard Herrmann; *Editor*: Alma Macrorie.

Cast: Edmund Gwenn (Captain Albert Wiles); John Forsythe (Sam Marlowe); Shirley MacLaine (Jennifer Rogers); Mildred Natwick (Miss Graveley); Mildred Dunnock (Mrs. Wiggs); Jerry Mathers (Arnie Rogers); Royal Dano (Calvin Wiggs); Parker Fennelly (The millionaire); Philip Truex (Harry).

The Man Who Knew Too Much (PARAMOUNT, 1956), COLOR, 120 MINUTES.

Producer: Alfred Hitchcock; *Associate Producer*: Herbert Coleman; *Screenplay*: John Michael Hayes (based on a story by Charles Bennett and D. B. Wyndham Lewis); *Director of Photography*: Robert Burks; *Assistant Director*: Howard Joslin; *Art Directors/Production Designers*: Hal Pereira and Henry Bumstead; *Set Designers*: Sam Comer and Arthur Krams; *Special Effects Supervisor*: John P. Fulton; *Wardrobe and Costumes*: Edith Head; *Music*: Bernard Herrmann; "Storm Cloud Cantata" by Arthur Benjamin and D. B. Wyndham Lewis; Songs, "Que Será, Será" and "We'll Love Again" by Jay Livingston and Ray Evans; *Editor*: George Tomasini.

Cast: James Stewart (Dr. Ben McKenna); Doris Day (Jo McKenna); Brenda de Banzie (Mrs. Drayton); Bernard Miles (Mr. Drayton); Daniel Gelin (Louis Bernard); Christopher Olsen (Hank McKenna); Reggie Nalder (Rien, the assassin); Ralph Truman (Buchanan); and: Mogens Wieth, Hilary Brooke, Carolyn Jones, Alan Mowbray, Richard Wattis, Alix Talton.

The Wrong Man (WARNER BROS., 1957), B&W, 105 MINUTES.

Producer: Alfred Hitchcock; *Associate Producer*: Herbert Coleman; *Screenplay*: Maxwell Anderson and Angus MacPhail (based on a story by Anderson); *Director of Photography*: Robert Burks; *Assistant Director*: Daniel J. McCauley; *Art Director/Production Designer*: Paul Sylbert; *Set Designer*: William L. Kuehl; *Music*: Bernard Herrmann; *Editor*: George Tomasini.

Cast: Henry Fonda (Christopher Emmanuel [Manny] Balestrero); Vera Miles (Rose Balestrero); Anthony Quayle (Frank O'Connor); Harold J. Stone (Lieutenant

Bowers); Nehemiah Persoff (Gene Conforti); Peggy Webber (Miss Dennerly); Esther Minciotti (Mrs. Balestrero); John Heldabrand (Tomasini); Doreen Lang (Mrs. James); Laurinda Barrett (Constance Willis); Norma Connolly (Betty Todd); Lola D'Annunzio (Olga Conforti); Robert Essen (Gregory Balestrero); Kippy Campbell (Robert Balestrero); Dayton Lummis (The judge); Charles Cooper (Detective Matthews); Richard Robbins (Daniel).

Vertigo (PARAMOUNT, 1958), COLOR, 128 MINUTES.

Producer: Alfred Hitchcock; *Associate Producer*: Herbert Coleman; *Screenplay*: Alec Coppel and Samuel Taylor (based on the novel *D'Entre les Morts* by Pierre Boileau and Thomas Narcejac); *Director of Photography*: Robert Burks; *Assistant Director*: Daniel McCauley; *Art Directors/Production Designers*: Hal Pereira and Henry Bumstead; *Set Designers*: Sam Comer and Frank McKelvey; *Titles*: Saul Bass; *Special Effects Supervisor*: John P. Fulton; *Special Sequence*: John Ferren; *Wardrobe and Costumes*: Edith Head; *Music*: Bernard Herrmann; *Editor*: George Tomasini.

Cast: James Stewart (John "Scottie" Ferguson); Kim Novak ("Madeleine Elster"/Judy Barton); Barbara Bel Geddes (Midge Wood); Tom Helmore (Gavin Elster); Konstantin Shayne (Pop Liebl); and: Henry Jones, Raymond Bailey, Ellen Corby, Lee Patrick.

North by Northwest (MGM, 1959), COLOR, 137 MINUTES.

Producer: Alfred Hitchcock; *Associate Producer*: Herbert Coleman; *Screenplay*: Ernest Lehman; *Director of Photography*: Robert Burks; *Art Directors/Production Designers*: Robert Boyle, William A. Horning, and Merrill Pye; *Set Designers*: Henry Grace and Frank McKelvey; *Titles*: Saul Bass; *Special Effects Supervisors*: A. Arnold Gillespie and Lee LeBlanc; *Music*: Bernard Herrmann; *Editor*: George Tomasini.

Cast: Cary Grant (Roger O. Thornhill); Eva Marie Saint (Eve Kendall); James Mason (Philip Vandamm); Jessie Royce Landis (Clara Thornhill); Leo G. Carroll (The professor); Philip Ober (Lester Townsend); Martin Landau (Leonard); Adam Williams (Valerian); Robert Ellenstein (Licht); and: Josephine Hutchinson, Doreen Lang, Les Tremayne, Philip Coolidge, Edward Binns, Pat McVey, Nora Marlowe, Ned Glass, Malcolm Atterbury.

Psycho (PARAMOUNT, 1960), B&W, 168 MINUTES.

Producer: Alfred Hitchcock; *Screenplay*: Joseph Stefano (based on the novel by Robert Bloch); *Director of Photography*: John L. Russell; *Assistant Director*: Hilton A.

Green; *Art Directors/Production Designers*: Joseph Hurley and Robert Clatworthy; *Set Designer*: George Milo; *Titles*: Saul Bass; *Special Effects Supervisor*: Clarence Champagne; *Wardrobe and Costumes*: Helen Colvig; *Music*: Bernard Herrmann; *Editor*: George Tomasini.

Cast: Anthony Perkins (Norman Bates); Janet Leigh (Marion Crane); Vera Miles (Lila Crane); John Gavin (Sam Loomis); Martin Balsam (Arbogast); John McIntire (Al Chambers); Lurene Tuttle (Mrs. Chambers); Simon Oakland (The psychiatrist); Frank Albertson (Cassidy); Patricia Hitchcock (Caroline); Vaughn Taylor (Mr. Lowery); Mort Mills (Highway patrolman); John Anderson ("California Charlie").

The Birds (UNIVERSAL, 1963), COLOR, 119 MINUTES.

Producer: Alfred Hitchcock; *Screenplay*: Evan Hunter (based on the short story by Daphne du Maurier); *Director of Photography*: Robert Burks; *Assistant Director*: James H. Brown; *Art Director/Production Designer*: Robert Boyle; *Titles*: James S. Pollak; *Set Designer*: George Milo; *Special Effects Supervisor*: Lawrence A. Hampton; *Special Photographic Adviser*: Ub Iwerks; *Pictorial Designs*: Albert Whitlock; *Bird Trainer*: Ray Berwick; *Wardrobe and Costumes*: Edith Head; *Electronic Sound Production and Composition*: Remi Gassman and Oskar Sala; *Musical Consultant*: Bernard Herrmann; *Editor*: George Tomasini; *Assistant to Alfred Hitchcock*: Peggy Robertson.

Cast: Tippi Hedren (Melanie Daniels); Rod Taylor (Mitch Brenner); Jessica Tandy (Lydia Brenner); Suzanne Pleshette (Annie Hayworth); Veronica Cartwright (Cathy Brenner); Ethel Griffies (Mrs. Bundy); Charles McGraw (Sebastian Sholes); Ruth McDevitt (Mrs. MacGruder); Malcolm Atterbury (Al Malone); Lonny Chapman (Deke Carter); Elizabeth Wilson (Helen Carter); Joe Mantell (The traveling salesman), Doodles Weaver (The fisherman); John McGovern (The postal clerk); Karl Swenson (The drunk); Richard Deacon (The man in the elevator); Doreen Long (The mother in Tides Cafe).

Marnie (UNIVERSAL, 1964), COLOR, 130 MINUTES.

Producer: Alfred Hitchcock; *Screenplay*: Jay Presson Allen (based on the novel by Winston Graham); *Director of Photography*: Robert Burks; *Assistant Director*: James H. Brown; *Art Director/Production Designer*: Robert Boyle; *Set Designer*: George Milo; *Pictorial Designs*: Albert Whitlock; *Wardrobe and Costumes*: Edith Head; *Music*: Bernard Herrmann; *Editor*: George Tomasini; *Assistant to Alfred Hitchcock*: Peggy Robertson.

Cast: Tippi Hedren (Margaret [Marnie] Edgar); Sean Connery (Mark Rutland); Diane Baker (Lil Mainwaring); Louise Latham (Bernice Edgar); Martin Gabel (Sidney Strutt); Bob Sweeney (Cousin Bob); Alan Napier (Mr. Rutland); Mariette Hartley

(Susan Clabon); Edith Evanson (Rita); S. John Launer (Sam Ward); Meg Wyllie (Mrs. Turpin); Bruce Dern (The sailor).

Torn Curtain (UNIVERSAL, 1966), COLOR, 125 MINUTES.

Producer: Alfred Hitchcock; *Screenplay*: Brian Moore; *Director of Photography*: John F. Warren; *Assistant Director*: Donald Baer; *Art Directors/Production Designers*: Hein Heckroth and Frank Arrigo; *Set Designer*: George Milo; *Pictorial Designs*: Albert Whitlock; *Wardrobe and Costumes*: Edith Head and Grady Hunt; *Music*: John Addison; *Editor*: Bud Hoffman; *Assistant to Alfred Hitchcock*: Peggy Robertson.

Cast: Paul Newman (Michael Armstrong); Julie Andrews (Sarah Sherman); Lila Kedrova (Countess Luchinska); Wolfgang Kieling (Gromek); Tamara Toumanova (The ballerina); Ludwig Donath (Professor Lindt); David Opatoshu (Jacobi); Gisela fisher (Dr. Koska); and: Mort Mills, Carolyn Conwell, Arthur Gould-Porter, Gloria Gorvin.

Topaz (UNIVERSAL, 1969), COLOR, 126 MINUTES.

Producer: Alfred Hitchcock; *Associate Producer*: Herbert Coleman; *Screenplay*: Samuel Taylor (based on the novel by Leon Uris); *Director of Photography*: Jack Hildyard; *Art Director/Production Designer*: Henry Bumstead; *Set Designer*: John Austin; *Wardrobe and Costumes*: Edith Head; *Music*: Maurice Jarre; *Editor*: William H. Ziegler; *Assistant to Alfred Hitchcock*: Peggy Robertson.

Cast: Frederick Stafford (André Dévereaux); John Forsythe (Michael Nordstrom); Dany Robin (Nicole Dévereaux); John Vernon (Rico Parra); Karin Dor (Juanita de Cordoba); Michel Piccoli (Jacques Granville); Philippe Noiret (Henri Jarre); Claude Jade (Michele Picard); Roscoe Lee Browne (Philippe Dubois); Per-Axel Arosenius (Boris Kusenov); Michel Subor (François Picard).

Frenzy (UNIVERSAL, 1972), COLOR, 116 MINUTES.

Producer: Alfred Hitchcock; *Associate Producer*: William Hill; *Screenplay*: Anthony Shaffer (based on the novel *Goodbye Piccadilly, Farewell Leicester Square* by Arthur La Bern); *Director of Photography*: Gil Taylor; *Assistant Director*: Colin M. Brewer; *Art Directors/Production Designers*: Syd Cain and Bob Laing; *Set Designer*: Simon Wakefield; *Music*: Ron Goodwin; *Editor*: John Jympson; *Assistant to Alfred Hitchcock*: Peggy Robertson.

Cast: Jon Finch (Richard [Dick] Blaney); Barry Foster (Bob Rusk); Barbara Leigh-Hunt (Brenda Blaney); Anna Massey (Babs Milligan); Alec McCowen (Inspector Oxford); Vivien Merchant (Mrs. Oxford); Billie Whitelaw (Hetty Porter); Clive

Swift (Johnny Porter); Bernard Cribbins (Felix Forsythe); Elsie Randolph (Gladys); Michael Bates (Sergeant Spearman); Jean Marsh (Monica Barling).

Family Plot (UNIVERSAL, 1976), COLOR, 120 MINUTES.

Producer: Alfred Hitchcock; *Screenplay*: Ernest Lehman (based on the novel *The Rainbird Pattern* by Victor Canning); *Director of Photography*: Leonard South; *Assistant Directors*: Howard G. Kazanjian and Wayne A. Farlow; *Art Director/Production Designer*: Henry Bumstead; *Set Designer*: James W. Payne; *Special Effects Supervisor*: Albert Whitlock; *Wardrobe and Costumes*: Edith Head; *Music*: John Williams; *Editor*: J. Terry Williams; *Assistant to Alfred Hitchcock*: Peggy Robertson.

Cast: Karen Black (Fran); Bruce Dern (George Lumley); Barbara Harris (Blanche Tyler); William Devane (Arthur Adamson); Ed Lauter (Maloney); Cathleen Nesbitt (Julia Rainbird); Katherine Helmond (Mrs. Maloney); Warren J. Kemmerling (Grandison); Edith Atwater (Mrs. Clay); William Prince (Bishop); Nicolas Colasanto (Constantine); Marge Redmond (Vera Hannagan).

videography

Birds, The: MCA Universal Home Video, 1998.

Blackmail: Hollywood Movie Greats, 1995.

Champagne: Valencia Entertainment Corp., 1989.

Dial M for Murder: Warner Bros. Home Video, Inc., 1991.

Easy Virtue: Hollywood Home Theatre, 1980.

Family Plot: MCA/Videocassette Inc., 1982.

Farmer's Wife, The: Republic Pictures Home Video, 1994.

Foreign Correspondent: Warner Bros. Home Video, Inc., 1991.

Frenzy: MCA Home Video, Inc., 1985.

I Confess: Warner Bros. Home Video, Inc., 1981.

Jamaica Inn: Valencia Entertainment Corp., 1989.

Juno and the Paycock: Valencia Entertainment Corp., 1989.

Lady Vanishes, The: Janus Films, 1985.

Lifeboat: Key Video/CBS/Fox Co., 1985.

Lodger: A Story of the London Fog, The: Hollywood Select Video, 1988.

Man Who Knew Too Much, The (1934): Valencia Entertainment Corp., 1989.

Man Who Knew Too Much, The (1956): MCA Home Video, Inc., 1984.

Manxman, The: Hollywood Home Theatre, 1986.

Marnie: MCA Universal Home Video, Inc., 1995.

Mr. and Mrs. Smith: The Nostalgia Merchant, Inc., 1983.

Murder: Republic Pictures Corp. & Lumiere Pictures, 1994.

North by Northwest: MGM/UA Home Video, 1990.

Notorious: CBS/Fox Video/ABC Video, Inc., 1998.

Number Seventeen: Republic Pictures Corp. & Lumiere Pictures, 1994.

Paradine Case, The: Key Video/ABC Video, Inc., 1975.

Psycho: Universal Home Video, Inc., 1997.

Rear Window: MCA Universal Home Video, Inc., 1990.

Rebecca: ABC Video, Inc., 1988.

Rich and Strange: Valencia Entertainment Corp., 1989.

Ring, The: Valencia Entertainment Corp., 1989.

Rope: MCA Home Video, Inc., 1989.

Sabotage: Hollywood Movie Greats, 1985.

Saboteur: MCA Home Video, Inc., 1985.

Secret Agent: Video Images, 1980.

Shadow of a Doubt: MCA Home Video, Inc., 1988.

Skin Game, The: Republic Pictures Corp. & Lumiere Pictures, 1994.

Spellbound: Twentieth Century-Fox Video/ABC Video, Inc./CBS/Fox Video, 1995.

Stage Fright: Warner Bros. Home Video Inc., 1990.

Strangers on a Train: Warner Bros. Home Video, Inc., 1998.

Suspicion: The Nostalgia Merchant, Inc., 1985.

39 Steps, The: Hollywood Movie Greats, 1985.

To Catch a Thief: Paramount Home Video, 1996.

Topaz: MCA Home Video, Inc., 1985.

Torn Curtain: MCA/Videocassette, Inc., 1984.

Trouble with Harry, The: MCA Home Video, Inc., 1995.

Under Capricorn: VidAmerica Inc., 1982.

Vertigo: MCA Home Video, Inc., 1984.

Wrong Man, The: Warner Bros. Home Video, Inc., 1989.

Young and Innocent: Hallmark Home Entertainment, 1995.

Alfred Hitchcock on the Internet

The Birds (American Film Institute's gallery of stills and production shots)
http://www.afionline.org/birds

Chaplin and Hitchcock
http://www.geocities.com/Hollywood/set/3921/index.html

The Definitive Alfred Hitchcock Links Page
http://www.interlog.com/~couke/index.html

The Films of Alfred Hitchcock
http://www.geocities.com/Athens/Oracle/6494/

The Hitchcock Aesthetic
http://www.soc.qc.edu/multimedia/Hitchcock/qesth.html

Hitchcock: The Master of Suspense
http://www.nextdch.mty.itesm.mx/~plopezg/Kaplan/Hitchcock.html

The Hitchcock Page
http://www.primenet.com/~mwc/awardshitch.html

Hitchcock Resource Guide
http://www.db.dk/student/k95/5/kfm/hitch.htm

"The MacGuffin" Web Page
http://www.labyrinth.net.au/~muffin

Bibliography

Anobile, Richard. A., editor. *Alfred Hitchcock's* Psycho. New York: Universe, 1974.

Ansen, David. "Dial R for Remake." *Newsweek*, June 15, 1998, p. 70.

Auiler, Dan. *Vertigo: The Making of a Hitchcock Classic*. New York: St. Martin's Press, 1998.

Baldwin, Kristen. "Where Are They Now?" *News Notes* 26, June 1998, p. 10.

Brestoff, Richard. *The Camera Smart Actor*. New Hampshire: Smith and Kraus, Inc., 1994.

Brill, Leslie. *The Hitchcock Romance: Love and Irony in Hitchcock's Films*. Princeton, NJ: Princeton University Press, 1988.

Burr, Ty. "The 50 Greatest Directors and Their 100 Best Movies." *Entertainment Weekly*, April 19, 1996, p. 19.

Chetwynd, Josh. "'Rear Window' cleaning begins." *Hollywood Reporter*, September 29, 1997, p. 26.

Desowitz, Bill. "Window Dressing." *Los Angeles Times*, September 28, 1997, Calendar section, pp. 28–30.

Durgnat, Raymond. *The Strange Case of Alfred Hitchcock*. Cambridge, MA: The M.I.T. Press, 1974.

Feeney, F. X. "Revival Pick of the Week." *Los Angeles Weekly*, December 20–26, 1996, Calendar section, p. 92.

Finler, Joel W. *Hitchcock in Hollywood*. New York: Continuum, 1992.

Freeman, David. *The Last Days of Alfred Hitchcock*. New York: Overlook, 1984.

Grove, Martin A. "Davis given more room to plot out his 'Murder.'" *Hollywood Reporter*, June 6, 1998, p. 14.

———. "'Fugitive' staff regroups for 'Perfect' WB crime." *Hollywood Reporter*, June 3, 1998.

———. "Hollywood Report: Warners carefully plots 'Perfect Murder' release." *Hollywood Reporter*, April 4, 1998.

Halley, Michael. *The Alfred Hitchcock Album.* Englewood Cliffs, NJ: Prentice Hall, 1981.

Harris, Robert A. and Michael Lasky. *The Films of Alfred Hitchcock.* Secaucus, NJ: Citadel Press, 1976.

Humphries, Patrick. *The Films of Alfred Hitchcock.* Greenwich, CN: Brom Books, 1986.

Kapsis, Robert E. *Hitchcock: The Making of a Reputation.* Chicago: University of Chicago Press, 1992.

Klady, Leonard. "Film Review—*A Perfect Murder.*" *Daily Variety*, June 1, 1998, p. 2.

LaValley, Albert. *Focus on Hitchcock.* Englewood Cliffs, NJ: Prentice-Hall, 1972.

Leahy, Michael. "You Can't Out-Hitchcock." *TV Guide*, April 16, 1988, p. 16.

Leff, Leonard J. *Hitchcock and Selznick.* New York: Weidenfeld & Nicolson, 1987.

Leitch, Thomas M. *Find the Director and Other Hitchcock Games.* Athens, GA: University of Georgia Press, 1991.

Lipper, Don. "Seek and You Shall Find: Brief Encounters." *Premiere*, April 1988, p. 11.

Maltin, Leonard. *The Disney Film—Third Edition.* New York: Hyperion, 1995.

Marton, Elise J. "Spellbinder." *Memories*, June/July 1990, pp. 75–80.

Modelski, Tania. *The Women Who Knew Too Much; Hitchcock and Feminist Theory.* New York: Methuen, 1988.

Moss, Marilyn. "Once You Meet A Stranger." *Hollywood Reporter*, September 25, 1996.

Natale, Richard. "Remaking the Master." *Los Angeles Times*, May 30, 1998, p. F1.

Perry, George. *The Films of Alfred Hitchcock.* New York: Dutton/Vista, 1965.

Phillips, Gene D. *Alfred Hitchcock.* Boston: Twayne, 1984.

Phillips, Louis. "The Hitchcock Universe: Thirty-Nine Steps and Then Some." *Films in Review*, March/April 1995, p. 22.

Price, Theodore. *Hitchcock and Homosexuality.* Lanhan, MD: Scarecrow Press, 1992.

Raubicheck, Walter and Walter Srebnick, editors. *Hitchcock's Re-released Films; From* Rope *to* Vertigo. Wayne, NE: Wayne State University Press, 1991.

Rebello, Stephen. *Alfred Hitchcock and the Making of* Psycho. New York: Dembner Books, 1990.

Rechtshaffen, Michael. "A Perfect Murder." *Hollywood Reporter*, June 1, 1998, p. 8.

Rohmer, Eric and Claude Chabrol. *Hitchcock: The First 44 Films*. New York: Ungar, 1979.

Rothman, William. *Hitchcock: The Murderous Gaze*. Cambridge, MA: Harvard University Press, 1982.

Ryall, Tom. *Alfred Hitchcock and the British Cinema*. Urbana, IL: University of Illinois Press, 1986.

Sauter, Van Gordon. "Television Reviews." *Daily Variety*, January 28, 1992, p. 15.

Schoell, William. *Stay Out of the Shower*. New York: Dembner Books, 1985.

Sharff, Stephan. *Alfred Hitchcock's High Vernacular*. New York: Columbia University Press, 1985.

Simone, Sam P. *Hitchcock as Activist: Politics and the War Films*. UMI Research Press, 1985.

Sinyard, Neil. *The Films of Alfred Hitchcock*. New York: Gallery Books, 1986.

Spoto, Donald. *The Art of Alfred Hitchcock—Fifty Years of His Motion Pictures*. New York: Doubleday, 1979.

———. *The Dark Side of Genus: The Life of Alfred Hitchcock*. Boston: Little Brown, 1983.

Taylor, John Russell. *Hitch: The Authorized Biography of Alfred Hitchcock*. London: Abacus, 1978.

Thomson, David. "Dating Vertigo." *Los Angeles Weekly*, October 25–31, 1996, p. 41.

Travers, Peter. "The Blonde That Got Away." *US*, November 1996, p. 49.

Truffaut, François. *Hitchcock/Truffaut*. New York: Simon & Schuster, 1983.

Tunison, Michael. "A Perfect Murder." *Entertainment Today*, June 5, 1998, p. 19.

Turan, Kenneth. "Still a Dizzying Experience." *Los Angeles Times*, October 13, 1996, p. 5.

Weiss, Elisabeth. *The Silent Scream: Alfred Hitchcock's Soundtrack*. Associated University Presses, 1982.

Willey, Mason and Bons, Damien. *Inside Oscar—The Unofficial History of the Academy Awards*. New York: Ballantine Books, 1986.

Wollen, Peter. "Compulsion." *Sight and Sound*, April 1997, p. 14.

Wood, Robin. *Hitchcock's Films*. London: A. S. Barnes, 1969.

———. *Hitchcock's Films Revisited*. New York: Columbia University Press, 1989.

Yacowar, Maurice. *Hitchcock's British Films*. Hamden, CN: Archon Books, 1977.

index

about the author

Kathleen Kaska is a teacher and author. Her first book, *What's Your Agatha Christie I.Q.?* was published in 1996. Kathleen is a die-hard mystery fan, and when she is not teaching and writing nonfiction, she is working on her own mysteries. Entering the world of fiction is a nice balance between dispersing factual information and letting the imagination run free.

Her second book, *The Alfred Hitchcock Triviography & Quiz Book,* is the result of her becoming a devoted Alfred Hitchcock fan in the 1960s when her parents finally extended her bedtime, allowing her to watch the weekly TV series, *Alfred Hitchcock Presents.* Hitchcock became her favorite fright factor after seeing his classic thriller *Psycho.* She has watched all of Hitchcock's available films, and many of them several times. As the result of her research, Ms. Kaska has ferreted out some interesting tidbits concerning the director's idiosyncrasies. She regards studying the work of Alfred Hitchcock an educational, as well as an enjoyable, endeavor.

Ms. Kaska lives in Austin, Texas, where she teaches seventh-grade science and freelances for various magazines.